# Shaker Architecture

*A Shaker Carpenter*

# Shaker Architecture

*Descriptions with Photographs and Drawings*
*of*
*Shaker Buildings*

**At**

Mount Lebanon, New York
Watervliet, New York
West Pittsfield, Massachusetts

**WILLIAM LAWRENCE LASSITER**

*Senior Curator of History and Art,*
*New York State Education Dept.*

*Illustrated by Constantine Kermes*

*BONANZA BOOKS · NEW YORK*

*TO*

*AMALIA MONTEMAYOR LASSITER*

*AND*

*MY SON*

*WILLIAM LAWRENCE LASSITER*

## FOREWORD

The Shakers were a religious group. But first of all, they were practical people. The movement had started in Manchester, England. Workers living in the slum areas of this factory town in the 1700's knew economic and moral conditions at their worst. No wonder they sought escape from the bonds and the ugliness of their physical daily lives. No wonder they sought escape to spiritual freedom and beauty. They found the latter first, under the leadership and inspiration of Ann Lee—"Mother Ann." It was not until she led them —a little band of eight followers—across the Atlantic to the port of New York that they also found economic freedom. It was like the admonition in the Bible; "Seek ye first the kingdom of God; and all these things shall be added unto you." But it was a long hard road from their first American home on a tract of wilderness land called Niskayuna (near Albany) before Shaker settlements in this county—the farmlands, the barns, the houses and the churches—became almost a pattern of perfection for the countryside about them.

The Shaker organization was comparatively simple. The Shakers were celibates, owning all things in common. Men and women were equal in power and responsibility. The little band of nine, grown to about six thousand by the middle 1800's, now occupied eighteen prosperous settlements scattered throughout New England, New York, Kentucky, and Ohio. Each separate community was governed by a Ministry consisting of two men and two women (elders and eldresses) who decided all matters of policy. These separate groups of leaders were answerable only to the central ministry at New Lebanon, New York. Thus it was possible to achieve uniformity throughout Shakerdom.

This accounts partly for the similarity of design and workmanship found in Shaker buildings and in furniture. But the absolute integrity of everything the Shakers made stems from three axioms left them by Mother Ann. First of all, she said to them: "Hands to work, and hearts to God." Then she laid down a principle which modern functionalists follow: "Every force evolves a form." And finally this advice: "Do all your work as though you had a thousand years to live, and as you would if you knew you must die tomorrow."

*Marguerite Fellows Melcher*

**SKETCH MAP of the SHAKER VILLAGE:**

COMPARATIVE DISTANCES WITHIN SHAKER VILLAGE LIMITS : MILES:

| A TO D | 1·65 | | A TO M | 1·20 | | A TO D | 1·65 |
|---|---|---|---|---|---|---|---|
| D TO SLM | ·80 | | M TO B | ·20 | | D TO M | ·40 |
| SLM TO P | ·90 | | B TO S | ·70 | | M TO S | ·90 |
| | | | S TO SLO | ·25 | | S TO SLO | ·25 |
| | | | SLO TO P | ·35 | | SLO TO P | ·35 |
| **MAIN ROAD** A·D·P | **3·35** MILES | | **OLD ROAD** A·M·P | **2·70** MILES | | **A·D·M·P** | **3·55** MILES |

ALBANY TO SHAKER VILLAGE State Line Monument 26 miles
ALBANY TO PITTSFIELD 36 miles   Monument TO PITTSFIELD 10 miles

About 2½ miles from Community Meeting House to WEST Family common

This Road led to Brickyard and to Shaker EAST Family : Buildings have been entirely torn down :

**NORTH FAMILY**

1 North Family Residence
2 Sales and Work Room
3 Ice Ho. Ice Bin
4 Chickens
5 Workshop
6 Laundry and Firewood with power
7 Brothers Quarters
8 Do. and Work rooms
9 - 10 Stores
11 Horses and Wagons
12 Storage
13 Workshops
14 North Barn - stone walls
15 East wing - wood
16 Centre wing wood
17 West wing wood
18 Workshops water power &c
19 Blacksmith Shop Trip hammer &c ox shoring
20 Water Power Mill wood sawing grist mill &c
21 Do. do.
22 Mill Pond. 23 Storage Reservoir :

**CHURCH FAMILY**
THESE BUILDINGS NOW UTILISED AS THE DARROW SCHOOL Lebanon.NY

1 Residence used as School ( Darrow School )
2 Meeting House of the Shaker Community erected 1822-1824
3 Museum ( Mint )
4 Workrooms (now Apartments)
5 Stand Principal Residence
6 Farm sheds
7 Garage
8 Workshops
9 Church made from Barn
10 Large Cattle & Hay barn
11 Sheds and Stores
12 Residence & Store &c
13 Residence
14 Garage
15 Cottage and Stores
16 Horse and Cattle Barns
17 Stores
18 Barn and Workshop
19 Stores
20 Water power 26 ft water wheel wood sawing and workshops grist mill &c

First Church bldg erected 1791:

SS = SHAKER SCHOOL: recently made over into cottage:

SHAKER COMMUNITY MEMORIAL

STORAGE RESERVOIR ¼ Mile

New State Road over Lebanon Mountain

State Road

TO PITTSFIELD

TO SHAKER VILLAGE

TO STEPHENTOWN

TO LEBANON SPRINGS

OLD ROAD

→ To Berkshire Farm Canaan and Chatham →

NEW LEBANON

TO ALBANY and P

+ Church with spire

Compiled - measured and drawn by A.K. Moseley Sept N.Y 1939

WORKS PROJECT ADMINISTRATION PROJECT 50470

Lebanon Mountain

NEW YORK and
MASSACHUSETTS
STATE LINE
MONUMENT

SLM

TO ALBANY N.Y.

TO PITTSFIELD Massachusetts

STATE LINE
N. 17° 36 E

STATE OF MASSACHUSETTS
STATE OF NEW YORK

N

To Hancock Shakers

To Pittsfield
26 Miles from Albany

SLO

**SOUTH FAMILY**

1 Center Family Residence
2 Do do
3 Cottage do
4 Site of burnt building
5 grass
6 Residence
7 Workshop
8 do do
9 do do
10 Barn & Cattle
11 Stores
12 Camp Barn
13 SOUTH WEST work cottage
14 Stores a

FAMILY

Water
Storage and
Aeration

**SOUTH FAMILY**

1 South Family Residence
2 Smaller Residence
3 Barn and Store
4 Residence
5 Do workshop
6 Do - Laundry 4th not
7 Large workshop chair factory
8 Stores
9 Stores
10 Stores - Chickens

11 Stores
12 Cattle Barn
13 Store Shed
14 Cattle and Hay
15 Do do
16 Do do
17 Camp Cottage
17 Residence

VILLAGE   ROAD

B

S

**SECOND FAMILY**

RESIDENCE NOW OCCUPIED BY
MEMBERS OF THE SECOND FAMILY
AND THE SOUTH FAMILY

1 Second Family Residence
2 Store
3 chair workshop now Store Residence
4 Storage sheds
5 Burnt Stone workshops
6 Cattle Barn etc.

15 Blacksmith Shop & Stores
with water power
Stone walls
16 Wagon storage

CEMETERY

CEMETERY

NOTE FROM THIS
LAKE ABOUT 1½ MILES
TO WEST FAMILY
SOME BUILDINGS
STILL EXIST. WERE
USUALLY KNOWN AS
THE CANAAN SHAKERS
(Note Lower Canaan family was
disbanded 1880. Upper Canaan
Family moved to Enfield Conn 1897.)

SKETCH OF
STATE LINE
MONUMENT AT
SLO ON THE
OLD ROAD
ALBANY TO
PITTSFIELD
THROUGH
SHAKER
VILLAGE.

1818
N. York
Mass.
Line.
26 M
From
Alby.

NOTE
THE LOWER
CANAAN FAMILY
DISBANDED 1884
BECAME THE BERKSHIRE
FARM for WAYWARD
BOYS.

# LEBANON: N.Y.
## Adjacent to the Massachusetts State Line:
### in COLUMBIA COUNTY
### NEW YORK STATE

# CONTENTS

FOREWORD

*By Margaret Fellows Melcher*

INTRODUCTION
*Page 13*

STONE BARN — NORTH FAMILY
*Page 25*

DWELLING HOUSE — NORTH FAMILY
*Page 32*

LAUNDRY BUILDING — NORTH FAMILY
*Page 45*

LUMBER AND GRIST MILL — NORTH FAMILY
*Page 52*

BRETHREN'S RED BRICK SHOP — NORTH FAMILY
*Page 58*

MEETING HOUSE — CHURCH FAMILY
*Page 65*

MINISTRY'S DWELLING HOUSE — CHURCH FAMILY
*Page 81*

BLACKSMITH'S SHOP — CHURCH FAMILY
*Page 88*

SHAKER SCHOOL — CHURCH FAMILY
*Page 93*

SISTERS' WORKSHOP — SOUTH FAMILY
*Page 99*

MAIN DWELLING HOUSE — WEST FAMILY
*Page 109*

"ROUND BARN" HANCOCK SHAKERS
*Page 123*

A SUGGESTED BIBLIOGRAPHY
*Page 127*

# LIST OF ILLUSTRATIONS

Frontispiece — *Shaker Carpenter*

*The Stone Barn* — Page 24

Stone Barn — Page 25

Dwelling House — Page 32

*Sisters' Room* — Page 33

Laundry Building — Page 45

*Sister Folding Towels* — Page 51

Lumber and Grist Mill — Page 52

*A Shaker Carpenter* — Page 57

Brethren's Red Brick Shop — Page 58

*In the Shoemaker's Shop* — Page 60

Meeting House — Page 65

*An entrance to the Meeting House* — Page 80

Ministry's Dwelling House — Page 81

*Members of the Ministry* — Page 83

Blacksmith's Shop — Page 88

*In the Blacksmith's Shop* — Page 89

Shaker School — Page 93

*The Schoolmaster and His Pupils* — Page 94

Sisters' Workshop — Page 99

*In the Sisters' Sewing Room* — Page 108

Main Dwelling House — Page 109

*Off-Center Double Doors* — Page 111

Round Barn — Page 123

*Inspiration Drawing* — Page 126

*INTRODUCTION*

In presenting these drawings and photographs it is proper to include a brief history of the Shakers, since all their designs of the buildings and artifacts were subordinate to their religious beliefs and established laws. The architectural designs — which are distinctive — evolved within the Shaker community and established a style, or a folk art in America.

A group of English Quakers led by James and Jane Wardley in Manchester, England, who had adopted some of the beliefs of the French Prophets, or Camisards of Vivarais and Dauphine, gave to the world a new religion which was to be known as the Shakers, or Believers in Christ's Second Appearing.

In 1758, Ann Lee (1736-1784), an illiterate woman, who was the daughter of a local blacksmith, joined this group and soon thereafter was proclaimed as the anointed one and replaced the Wardleys as leader. She was regarded as the female expression of the Christ Spirit, and Jesus of Nazareth as the male expression of that spirit.

In 1774, while a prisoner in the Manchester jail for breaking the Sabbath by her noisy songs and shouts, she reported to her followers upon her release that she had received a visit from Jesus who directed her to take her followers to the North American Colonies, where they would be able to practice and propagate their faith unmolested. This was accomplished through the generosity of John Hocknell (1723-1799), a member who had funds, and who agreed to pay for the voyage of those who cared to sail for North America.

Only nine persons chose to venture across the Atlantic on the old and unsafe ship, the *Mariah*. They left England on May 19, 1774, and by some miracle arrived in New York on Sunday afternoon, August 6, 1774. After a short residence in New York City, where the members followed various occupations, they decided to change their home to a secluded place.

John Hocknell went to Albany, New York, and acquired land in the wilderness in Niskayuna (now known as West Albany or Watervliet) from Squire Stephen Van Rensselaer, Lord of the Manor of Rensselaerwyck. Here the Shakers cleared and drained the swamp lands, and built log cabins. It was here they suffered physical privation from hunger and cold, but they were free to practice their religious beliefs without interference.

It was not until Joseph Meacham, Talmadge Bishop, and Calvin Harlow — who were the leaders of a group of revivalists at Mount Lebanon, New York — went to Niskayuna to investigate the Believers' faith that the general public began hearing about the "Shaking Quakers." This group of revivalists again sent their emissaries to Niskayuna to investigate and, like Meacham, Bishop, and Harlow, returned to Mount Lebanon to declare that it was the most satisfying of all faiths they had known, and that these Shakers were the true disciples of the faith they had long sought.

Mother Ann Lee, and Father William Lee (1743-1784), a brother of Mother Ann, went to Mount Lebanon on invitation to tell of their beliefs and to preach their gospel. This was, in fact, the beginning of a proselyting journey in New York and the New England states that took them to thirty-six towns. Men and women "gathered in like doves"; husbands and wives and their children embraced this new faith, and those divided in opinion separated and went their own way.

It was this separation of the families and the Shaker preachment of the celibate life that brought persecution and prosecution to the group. Their enemies accused them of trying to annihilate the human race and of being English spies. The leaders, including Mother Ann, were thrown into the jails of Albany and Poughkeepsie but were freed when no just reason for their imprisonment was established. In 1784, both Mother Ann Lee (1743-1784), and Father William Lee (1736-1784), died as a result of mob attacks upon them on a trip through New England. Their deaths were deemed as sacrifices for the faith, and the converts determined to establish their faith more firmly.

The cardinal principles of Shakerism were celibacy, community of goods, confession of sins, and withdrawal from the world. On these principles, the pioneers and those who followed them built their own environment — Paradise on earth.

The Shaker Society was organized at Mount Lebanon, New York, in 1788. It was here that the members came to live in a community where they could worship and work together, and be free from the interference of the world's people. Within this community the Millennial Laws were formulated by Father Joseph Meacham, the first American convert, and Mother Lucy Wright. These laws explained what was and what was not in the Gospel Order, for both personal conduct and communal administration. These laws guided not only the Mount Lebanon Society, but also all the societies established thereafter.

There were nineteen Shaker Societies established in the United States, and just before the Civil War the membership numbered about six thousand.

The Shaker government was vested in Christ and in his human representatives, a dual order of leaders. The ministry consisted of brethren and sisters whose special duty was to guide and superintend the spiritual concerns of the Society, and to cooperate with the elders and eldresses, who protected the spiritual affairs of their own families. The temporal affairs were cared for by the trustees, deacons and deaconesses. All of these leaders were accountable to the Central Ministry, which was located at the Church Family, Mount Lebanon, New York.

From 1790 to just before the Civil War, within the Shaker Society, manufacturing, agriculture and invention were at their greatest height. Agricultural products were produced in such abundance that the trustees were forced to find a market for those commodities which exceeded home consumption. Shaker brethren, therefore, were familiar figures selling their wares in the local market places, the streets of the cities, towns and villages near Shaker settlements.

Their garden seed business, begun about 1789, made them the first to commercialize this product. This was one of the most lucrative businesses carried on in several of the Shaker communities. This business passed out of existence when the world's business men entered the field with great financial investments and advertising.

At Mount Lebanon, New York, the medicinal herb business was started about 1800. Under the leadership of competent botanists, Brother Elias Harlow and Brother Barnabas Hinckley, this business grew rapidly. Not only were herbs assorted and packaged, but extracts, powders, essential oils, salves, syrup compounds, and pills were sold all over the world to druggists and physicians.

Many other products were made in the Shaker shops in the various communities, such as tinware for dairy and kitchen uses, leather shoes, boots, harnesses, and hats. From the sisters' shops came such products as all kinds of woolen cloth, linen cloth, fans, cloaks, canned fruits and vegetables, and also baskets. To this list could be added many other products.

Shaker oval boxes and chairs epitomize Shaker plainness and beauty. The beauty was created by making these objects "functional," because starting out to design a beautiful object was "not in order"; in the Shaker view beauty was a snare of the devil, and the Millennial Laws forbade the Believers to create beauty for beauty's sake.

The oval boxes were general utility boxes and often came in nests of twelve, the smallest being about three inches long and two inches high, and the largest about fifteen inches long and eight inches high. They were made of maple and pine.

The chairs, both straight chairs and rockers, were of a simple New England slat-back type. The rockers were made with and without arms. The straight chairs, sometimes called "tilting chairs," had the rear post terminating with a pine cone finial, without imitation carving. The rear post of most of the "tilting" chairs was fitted with a special Shaker invention — the ball and socket in the lower rear post. The ball, flattened on the floor end, was attached in the socket by leather thongs. This device, known among the Shakers as a "Casidomia" (derived from the Spanish—*casi*—almost, and *domia*—asleep) prevented slipping and also damaging the floor or carpet. The South Family at Mount Lebanon, New York, were known as the champion chairmakers of the world (Manifesto, July 1895).

There are many inventions known to be of Shaker origin, and many others are in use today but not generally attributed to these people. A few of the common objects of Shaker invention in use today are metallic pens, clothespins, apple-parers, one-horse wagons, and flat corn brooms. It was Sister Tabitha Babbit, of the Harvard, Massachusetts, Society, who is accredited with the invention of the circular saw. ("Gleaning from Old Shaker Journals" by Clara E. Sears, 1916; *"Simonds Guide for Millmen,"* Simonds Manufacturing Company, Vol. XIV, No. 2, March-April 1922.)

As late as sixty years ago it was not an uncommon sight to see the Shaker sisters and brethren walking through the streets of nearby cities and villages; as in Albany, New York; Harvard, Massachusetts; Concord, New Hampshire, and Pittsfield, Massachusetts. They had many business errands to perform in these places, where they solicited and delivered orders for products of the Shaker farms and shops. They were identifiable by their dress.

The sisters wore long dresses with wide pleated skirts, and a plain bodice, over which was draped a cotton or silk neckerchief which was folded and pinned at the belt to form a bertha. The head covering was a poke bonnet of woven straw, or of quilted cloth. A cape, about five inches broad and made of a thin cloth, was sewn to the back edge of this bonnet, to protect the neck from the sun in summer and from the cold in winter.

During the colder months of the year the sisters wore a circular cape fitted with a hood that covered the bonnet if desired. These capes were made of gray, black, and brown broadcloth.

The original costume for women was adopted from the antique style in vogue at the time of the inception of the organization. The designing of this original uniform has been attributed to Mother Lucy Wright, but changes in this attire have been made during the past seventy years.

The brethren's costume for working in the shops and in the fields consisted of loose trousers and a smock of unbleached or bleached coarse linen. The hats, all Shaker-made, were broad-brimmed with high crowns. For Sundays the suits were made of fine woven materials of wool, or wool-and-cotton mixture. A vest was worn over a white shirt, and over this a long frock coat of the same color or of a lighter hue. The winter overcoat, or surtout, was a fitted long coat with a shoulder cape. The colors of these coats were gray, dark blue, tan, or black.

In 1849, Elder Harvey L. Eads of South Union, Kentucky, published his *"Tailor's Division System,"* illustrated with eighteen plates and three additional plates of diagrams, which made for a more uniform dress among the brethren.

The shoes for both brethren and sisters were made by the Shaker cobblers, and usually had handwoven cloth tops with leather heels and soles.

Many theories have been projected as to the cause of the decline of the Shaker organization, or Believers in Christ's Second Appearing, but certainly no single one of them can be accepted as conclusive. To those not familiar with the social and economic history of this period, the celibate restrictions placed upon Shaker members would naturally seem to be the one and only reason. Celibacy was not even the dominant reason, but it was, without any doubt, a contributing factor. The Believers approved of marriage and procreation for the world's people but not for themselves, for they were of a higher spiritual order and intended to follow the life of Jesus Christ, whose life was one of continence.

During and after the Civil War there was a sharp decline in the membership, especially among the male population. During the war young men and women, who might have joined the Shaker Society, entered into other pursuits; the young men joined the Army, and the young women entered into business or industry. After the war the rapid industrialization that took place in the North, the South, and the West lured men and women into the factories and offices; the trek westward from the east in search of gold and homesteading, also drew prospective members from the Shaker fold.

The "deserving female" converts no longer swelled the ranks as they had twenty years before the Young Women's Christian Association in New York City opened a training class in typewriting for young women. Classes in other cities were opened and soon "the female typewriters" were in demand. The social stigma against working women was abolished, and young women and widows left alone in the world went into offices to earn an independent living — they no longer sought the Shakers for protection and security.

Men and women who had been in the Shaker Society withdrew at an alarming rate because they no longer had the "calling" for the Shaker way of life. And, too, state laws were instituted which regulated the adoptions and education of children, and the establishing of orphan asylums by other religious groups and governments diminished the numbers taken into the "Children's Order." The Shakers not only enjoyed having children to care for and train, but hoped that many would stay among them when they reached the age of twenty-one years and would then choose to sign the Covenant of their own volition.

All Shaker societies suffered during the Civil War, especially those in Kentucky, which never recovered from the loss sustained from the marauding Union and Confederate troops. The northern societies stood by and saw their once large and lucrative enterprises shrink and disappear before their eyes. The very industries, which they had started shortly after their organization in 1788, were taken by the "world's people" who had large funds to invest and were willing to take a gambler's chance in order to reap large financial returns with cheap labor, machinery and extensive advertising. The investors were rewarded with large profits. The Shakers could not compete with the low selling prices of the finished machine products of the outside manufacturer.

Some members blamed the friction that took place in the organization as the fatal blow. The fission separated the group into two parts, which weakened the structure of the Society. A conservative group headed by Elder Harvey Eads of Kentucky and Elder Henry Blinn of the New Hampshire group believed that the Shaker should adhere strictly to the principles of Mother Ann Lee in regard to living apart from the world's people. On the other side of the chasm was the liberal group led by Elder Frederick Evans of Mount Lebanon, New York, who advocated that Shakers should take an active part in world affairs. Evans and his liberal group dominated, thus creating an organization divided against itself. Elder Frederick grew more obdurate as he grew older and had things his way until his last days.

A middle group arose and was led by Eldress Lelia Taylor and Eldress Anna White, but the fissure could not be closed—it was too wide and too deep.

In later years the business affairs of the Shaker Society were greatly harmed by mismanagement by those who had taken over. The Shakers were not properly prepared to assume responsibility, since they had not been trained to the revolutionary changes that had taken place in the world's business and commerce, and consequently suffered great financial losses.

Summing up all of these social and economic changes that have brought to near-extermination the oldest of the socio-religious groups in the United States, it can only be said that the Shakers have made great contributions to the United States and to civilization. Marguerite Fellows Melcher, author of *The Shaker Adventure,* states in a letter to the writer that "Everything in this world — from flowers to civilization — seems to fade, decline from its moment of most perfect fulfillment. Why? Maybe it is a law of the universe."

Nineteen Shaker Societies were established in the United States, and during their heyday there were about six thousand members. Today there are two Societies left: one at Canterbury, New Hampshire, and the other at

Sabbath Day Lake, Maine. The total membership is twenty-two. There are no living Brethren.

During the great "ingathering" of members and communal prosperity, which occurred between 1790-1864, all Shaker settlements launched an overwhelming building program. During this time new dwelling houses and shops were erected or old ones remodeled for the convenience and comfort of the increasing membership. With combined efforts of the master builders, masons, stonecutters, bricklayers, lumber workers, and blacksmiths those buildings that are still standing were constructed according to the Gospel Order, or the rules concerning building set down in the Millennial Laws.

At this time the Shakers had among them men of much experience in construction work. From the Shaker *Manifesto,* the monthly journal, autobiographies and biographies, research discloses that "master builders," or architects, possessed extraordinary ability, and what is left for inspection attests to this claim. Elder Giles Avery at Mount Lebanon, New York, was a famed carpenter; Elder Harvey Eads of South Union, Kentucky, was not only a skilled carpenter, but a most versatile man in other trades as well. Micajah Burnett at Pleasant Hills was an experienced architect and builder before joining the Shakers, as was Elder Moses Johnson of Enfield, New Hampshire, who was a master builder of Meeting Houses. Added to this list was Elder George Wickersham who, as a youth, and before joining the Shakers, was a builder.

The buildings at Mount Lebanon, New York, served as models for other communities established later. Master builders from the Shaker village at Mount Lebanon often went to the newly-established settlements to supervise and assist in the construction work of newly-formed communities.

In the dwelling houses were the "retiring rooms" (or bedrooms), the kitchens, bake-rooms, food storage rooms and dining rooms. Here also was the "Meetings Room," where the "family" assembled in the evening for a religious service; to discuss the business and work program for the next day, and to hear a report on world affairs by those who had been assigned to read the current newspapers and periodicals. This room was equipped with either chairs or benches and was usually located on the first floor, but sometimes on the second floor.

The retiring rooms were on the first floor and the floors above. Each room was spacious enough to accommodate from three to four single beds. Built-in or movable chests of draws and cupboards were ample to accommodate the belongings of those who occupied a room. Adjoining each retiring room was a dressing room in which there were several "wash-sinks" with their own bowls and pitcher sets, towel racks, and peg boards for hanging up clothing.

In the basement were the dining rooms for the family and the guests. The large family dining room was entered by separate doors for the sisters and brethren. They sat at separate tables and at opposite ends of the room, near their respective entrances. Around the room, as in every other room, was a row of peg boards, on which each person hung his or her chair at the conclusion of each meal. This facilitated the cleaning of the tables and floors by those in charge of the dining room. The built-in cupboards and chests of drawers were ample to accommodate the large quantities of china, glass, silverware and linens. In the dining room, near the china cupboards, was a sink with drainboards for washing glass, china, and silverware used at meal times.

Adjoining the dining room was the kitchen, separated by a double door to allow free passage for those who replenished the serving dishes. Both doors remained open during the meal hours.

The location of the kitchen range determined the placing of other conveniences, such as tables, counters, shelves, and sinks. The cook's counter was opposite the stove. The top half near the dining room was made of wood; the other half, near the kitchen sink, was stone. The wooden portion of the top was for the serving dishes; and the stone portion for pots and pans that could be lifted directly from the stove. In this way there was no damage to chinaware, and no burning of the table top from pots and pans.

A counter near the cooling room, or refrigerator room, was the spot to which the left-over food from the dining room was returned. Cupboards under this counter, or nearby, accommodated the vessels used for storing the left-over food from the dining room and kitchen. A few steps from this counter was the "cooling-room."

The cooling room was paved with slabs of marble or blue flagstone. Here were tables with stone tops, and stone basins partly filled with water in which crocks or earthenware containers with food were placed. Basins of stone held large blocks of ice or, as in the case of the room in the North Family, Mount Lebanon, New York, water from the springs in the mountain which circulated through pipes that surrounded the walls. No ice was required in this room.

The bake-room on the same floor and often adjoining the kitchen had its own especially designed brick oven, arch kettles, and sinks. There were a few standing pieces, such as wooden and stone-top tables, flour bins, and tables for cutting bread. Conveniently placed on the walls were hanging cupboards and shelves for supplies. Adjacent to this room was a pan and supply room.

The canning and preserving kitchen with its storeroom was remote from the other kitchen and bake-rooms. It too was equipped with special arch kettles, sinks, counters, tables, hanging cupboards for condiments, and small equipment used in canning. The storeroom for the canned goods was under this kitchen, which made it possible to have a "lift" or dumbwaiter from the kitchen to this subterranean room. The jars and crocks with preserved food were placed on stone-topped tables or on counters placed around the room, which was rodent-and insect-proof. The floor, paved with slabs of bluestone at a depth below ground was always cool during the warmest days of summer.

The attics of all Shaker dwelling houses were completely finished. Some of them were divided into rooms and had built-in cases of drawers and cupboards.

The floors, if not in a natural finish, were stained a reddish yellow, and the floor boards were narrow or wide, depending on the era in which the building was erected.

The walls were plain plaster and painted white, or cerulean blue, which is often called "Shaker blue"; some were light tan. The woodwork in the room was a natural finish or ochre yellow.

It will be noted upon inspection of the drawings that because of the physical location of kitchens, dining rooms, bake-rooms, and storerooms, there was no reason for the workers to leave the confines of their respective working areas.

The shops, of course, showed greater variations in plan than the dwelling houses. Designed for particular occupations, they necessarily differed in arrangement. Workbenches and storage cabinets were placed so as to avoid lost motion by the artisan and to provide him with a maximum of comfort and safety. The location of a shop within a building was always carefully planned. If the occupation required a hoist or an elevator such was placed in the room, or nearby, in order to reduce handling; whether the doors were double or off center, was also determined by the bulk of the raw material to be brought in and the size of the finished products going out.

The exteriors of all buildings were plain and well proportioned, without embellishment that added nothing to the structural purity which gave eminence to Shaker architecture. All structures in a Shaker village, both inside and outside, reflected the lives of the people who lived and worked in them.

The great barns at Canterbury, New Hampshire; Mount Lebanon, New York; Pittsfield (Hancock), Massachusetts, and Watervliet (Niskayuna) New York, upon examination show that much labor and forethought were projected for the care and treatment of the farm animals. The Millennial Law, Section VII, No. 4 was obeyed in planning all Shaker barns for "No beast belonging to the people of God may be left to suffer with hunger, thirst, or cold, in consequence of neglect, on the part of those who have the care of them, but all should be kept in proper places and properly attended to according to their needs."

The silos, grain bins and hay mows were filled to provide bountiful supply for all animals over the most prolonged period from summer to spring. The construction of barns was tight and properly ventilated, and every device possible was made to insure a clean and sanitary condition. The architectural drawings of the barns at the North Family, Mount Lebanon, New York, and the "round" barn at Pittsfield, Massachusetts, show this.

The reader's attention is called to the use made of the hillsides in constructing a barn and other structures. By taking advantage of the natural topography, the various levels of a barn could be entered easily into and without bridges, which were expensive to build as well as to maintain.

Since they were chiefly an agrarian group, much attention was paid to planning a barn by the master builders.

The architectural drawings reproduced here and supplemented by photographs show a distinctive style of structure that evolved within the Believers' communities. Architectural designs, as all other forms in the community ,were subordinate to the Millennial Laws that guarded the Shaker master builder or architect against any styles or devices he may have employed out in the "world." However, during the last quarter of the nineteenth century when the Shaker male population was greatly reduced outside builders were hired to assist in construction work, especially when the project was too enormous for the brethren to undertake alone. Deviations from pure Shaker buildings are noticed where outside builders were employed. Outstanding examples are the dwelling house and the Ministry's residence at the Church Family, Mount Lebanon, New York, erected after the great fire of 1875.

In Kentucky, regional differences in architecture are reflected in some of the buildings. However, the majority of these structures are basically Shaker-influenced.

There are many unique features about Shaker buildings that made them different from others. The interior wall treatment, the floor and woodwork, the windows, the ubiquitous peg boards, the stair rails, doors, hardware, door canopies without external supports, hand rails, boot scrapers on the steps, and the plain but beautiful exterior gave charm not only to a building but to the entire Shaker community. Even today, when the buildings are occupied by groups alien to the Shaker belief, there is a great spiritual feeling of peace that pervades an entire Shaker village.

The drawings herewith presented were produced by the Works Progress Administration's New York State Museum Project Number 50470, during the economic recession of 1929-1941. The late Charles C. Adams, Director of the New York State Museum, and Andrew Delahanty, Supervisor of the United States Government Historical Building Survey, selected the buildings to be measured because they were the most representative and important structures left in the Shaker communities at Watervliet, Albany County, New York; Mount Lebanon, Columbia County, New York; and Pittsfield (West Pittsfield or Hancock), Berkshire County, Massachusetts. A few of these buildings that were measured during the survey are no longer extant, and many of those existing have undergone changes to meet the requirements of the present owners. These vicissitudes, combined with disuse and the destructive forces of the natural elements, have in many cases played havoc in these once model Shaker communities.

Collections of Shaker materials and literature are to be found in the New York State Library at Albany, New York; Western Reserve Historical Society, Cleveland, Ohio; Shaker Heights Historical Society, and the Shaker Heights Savings Association at Shaker Heights, Ohio; Golden Lamb Inn, Lebanon, Ohio; Dartmouth College Museum and Library at Hanover, New Hampshire; Fruitlands and Wayside Museum, Harvard, Massachusetts; Shaker Museum, Old Chatham, New York; Williams College Library, Williamstown, Massachusetts; Grosvenor Library, Buffalo, New York; New York Public Library, New York; The Library of Congress, Washington, District of Columbia; School of Religion, State University of Iowa, Iowa City, Iowa; Francis DuPont Winterthur Museum, Winterthur, Delaware; Hancock Shaker Village, Hancock, Massachusetts; Shaker Museum, Auburn, Kentucky; Pleasant Hill at Old Shakertown Incorporated, Shakertown, Kentucky, and the New York State Museum at Albany.

The watercolor renderings of the Shaker objects made by the Works Progress Administration's artist between 1927-1937 are in the Federal Index of Design, National Art Gallery, Washington, D. C. The architectural drawings and the photographs used in this publication are in the collections of the Historic American Building Survey, Library of Congress, Washington, D.C. These are of great importance to research students, especially those interested in Shaker folk arts and designs.

Many thanks are given to Professor Lionel Wyld, Dr. Frederick H. Bair, Miss Estella Weeks, Mrs. Ethel Hotaling Drumm, and Mrs. Marguerite Fellows Melcher for their help and invaluable criticism.

I am indebted to the Library of Congress for the use of the architectural drawings and the photographs from the permanent collections, all of which were made under the Works Progress Administration 1929-1941.

To Constantine Kermes who made the illustrations for this book, and Mrs. Marion Bollman Bender who handled the typing of the manuscript, I am most grateful.

*William Lawrence Lassiter*

Albany, New York, 1962

*The Stone Barn*

### STONE BARN: NORTH FAMILY, MOUNT LEBANON, NEW YORK

The great stone barn was completed in 1858, under the supervision of Elder George Wickersham, the designer. His original plans of this building (New York State Museum's Historical Catalog Number 6248) are in the Shaker Collection at the New York State Museum.

The dimensions are 196 feet long by 50 feet wide. There are five floors in all, three of which — the first, second and fourth — may be entered by doors that open at their level on the hillside, thus eliminating bridges. The original flat roof was removed some years after construction and replaced by a gable roof covered with slate, to prevent the accumulation of snow which would have added to the weight.

*Stone Barn*

PLAN of MIDDLE FLOOR of NORTH BARN
Scale 16 feet to 1 Inch;

Oxen will draw to deliver and Store Hay from above.

SILO

Oxen will draw to deliver and Store Hay from above.

SILO

SILO

SCALES

HISTORIC AMERICAN BUILDINGS SURVEY
SHEET 2 OF 5 SHEETS

PART DETAIL OF 4 WAY (FIXED) CARDINAL POINTS.

SKETCH OF FINIAL TO LANTERN VANE Etc.

MIDDLE STORY used as HAY MOW.

DRIVE WAY FLOOR

CATTLE FLOOR ON THE GROUND.

PART LONG SECTION:
Scale 8 feet to 1 Inch.

SIDE WALL AT ROOF WITH OVERHANG OF EAVES (approximate)

TYPICAL WINDOW:

HEAD

JAMB

CROSS SECTION:
Scale 8 feet to 1 Inch.

MIDDLE FLOOR PLAN AND SECTIONS

NORTH STONE BARN

Stone Barn North Family of Shakers Lebanon Columbia County N.Y.

NAME OF STRUCTURE

A.K. Hadley, del
Troy N.Y. 1940

UNDER DIRECTION OF UNITED STATES DEPARTMENT OF THE INTERIOR
NATIONAL PARK SERVICE, BRANCH OF PLANS AND DESIGN

On the lower floor, west elevation, the refuse pits are located; this made it possible for wagons to be driven in and out through the two broad doorways.

On the east end lies the entrance to the fourth floor from the main Shaker road. The large sliding doors admitted a team of horses with a loaded hayrack. At the west end of this floor space was arranged so that the team, after unloading the hayrack into the self-leveling hay mow, could turn around and leave by the same east door through which the team had entered. At this entrance, on the east end and on both sides, are the openings for filling the built-in silos.

On the south side are attached wooden buildings, open cattle sheds, and sheds for farm implements, which project into a fenced cattle yard.

This structure is reputed to be the largest all-stone barn in the United States.

SOUTH ELEVATION
of NORTH STONE BARN:

TIE ROD
BOLTS

TOP FLOOR
DRIVEWAY
FOR UNLOADING 2
HORSE WAGON LOADS
OF HAY ETC:

Driveway Floor - Entered
at East End of Barn from the
Shaker Village Road.

NOTE. FLOOR OMIT?
ALONG BOTH SIDEWALLS
FOR HAY MOW. MIDDLE
FLOOR CLEAR TO ROOF

NOTE AS TO 4½
CENTER SIDEWALL BAYS

PLANK FLOOR WITH 5
JOISTS ARE OMITTED AND
MAIN BEAMS STOPPED AT
* AS OPEN WELL - THUS
ALLOWING HAY STORAGE
FULL HEIGHT. MIDDLE
FLOOR CLEAR UP TO ROOF

HAY MOW
PROVIDES HAY STORE
FROM MIDDLE FLOOR
UP TO ROOF. OVER
100 FT. LENGTHWISE
SIMILAR NORTH SIDE

MIDDLE FLOOR
GANGWAY -
preparing Cattle feed
chop. roots. silage &c
ready to be passed
down to Cattle:

HAY MOW
PROVIDES HAY STORE
FROM MIDDLE FLOOR
UP TO ROOF - FOR 108
FEET LENGTHWISE
ALSO SAME SOUTH SIDE

SKELETON SECTION SKETCH OF THE
NORTH STONE BARN  NORTH FAMILY OF
SHAKERS LEBANON NY
- SCALE 4 FEET TO ONE INCH -

A.H. Mosher
N.Y.  meas. & dell.
1940-1948.  APPROXIMATE GRADE OF ROAD AT LOWEST POINT WEST END TO TAKE MANURE TO FIELDS

DOORS                    DOORS

5

## DWELLING HOUSE: NORTH FAMILY, MOUNT LEBANON, NEW YORK

A five-story basement and subbasement building, this dwelling was erected in 1818. The north end was added in 1846.

Like many Shaker buildings, this house was constructed in order to take advantage of the topography. The south subbasement has the furnace room, store room, brethren's wash room, and a storage room. The north subbasement has the cold cellars for the storage of preserved foods.

The basement, which is one flight down from the main east entrance, accommodates the kitchens, bakery, family dining room, guest dining room, hired men's dining room, pantries, store rooms, and the refrigerator room. The cooling or refrigerator room, a forerunner of our modern walk-in refrigerator rooms, is encircled with pipes through which circulated the cold water from a spring-fed reservoir. It served the North Family from the day of its installation to the day the remaining members migrated over the mountain to the Pittsfield Shaker farm in 1947.

In this building are the radiators and the ventilating systems devised by Elder Frederic Evans (1808-1893), noted scholar and Shaker leader.

The windows, doors, hardware, and arch kettles represent excellent examples of Shaker ingenuity and craftsmanship.

*Dwelling House*

*Sister's Room*

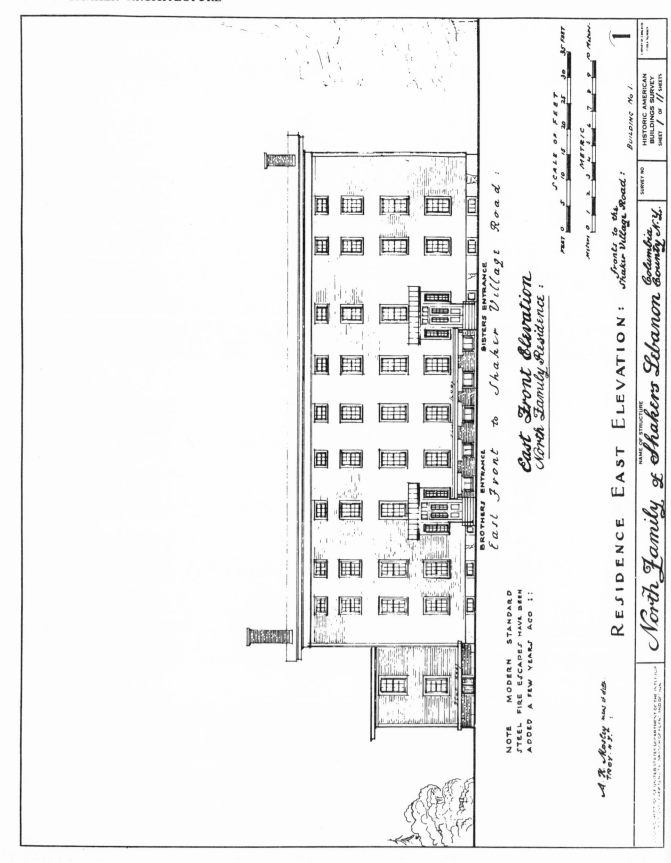

NOTE MODERN STANDARD
STEEL FIRE ESCAPES HAVE BEEN
ADDED A FEW YEARS AGO !!

A. R. Motley M.N.Y.S.D.D.B.
TROY, N.Y.

BROTHERS ENTRANCE          SISTERS ENTRANCE

East Front to Shaker Village Road :

East Front Elevation
North Family Residence :

SCALE OF FEET
FEET 0    5    10   15   20  25   30   35 FEET
METRIC
METERS 0   1   2   3   4   5   6   7   8   9   10 METERS

BUILDING No 1.

RESIDENCE EAST ELEVATION :   Front to the
Shaker Village Road :

North Family of Shakers Lebanon Columbia County N.Y.

| SURVEY NO | NAME OF STRUCTURE | HISTORIC AMERICAN BUILDINGS SURVEY SHEET 1 OF 11 SHEETS |
| --- | --- | --- |

1

LIBRARY OF CONGRESS HABS NUMBER

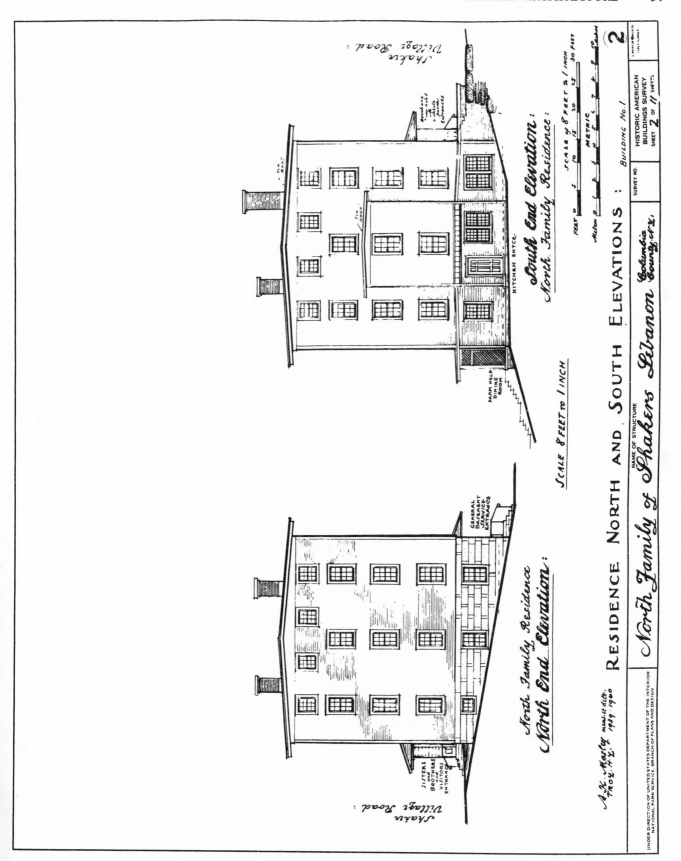

Shaker Village Road:

South End Elevation:
North Family Residence:

KITCHEN ENTCE.

FARM HELP.
DINING
ROOM

SCALE 8 FEET to 1 INCH

North Family Residence
North End Elevation:

Shaker Village Road:

SUTERS and BROTHERS and VISITORS ENTRANCE

GENERAL BASEMENT SERVICE ENTRANCE

RESIDENCE NORTH AND SOUTH ELEVATIONS: North Family of Shakers Lebanon Columbia County N.Y.

NAME OF STRUCTURE

SURVEY NO.

BUILDING No.1

HISTORIC AMERICAN BUILDINGS SURVEY
SHEET 2 OF 11 SHEETS

UNDER DIRECTION OF UNITED STATES DEPARTMENT OF THE INTERIOR
NATIONAL PARK SERVICE BRANCH OF PLANS AND DESIGN

SCALE of 8 FEET to 1 INCH
30 FEET

FEET 0    5    10    15    20    25

METRIC

Meters

2

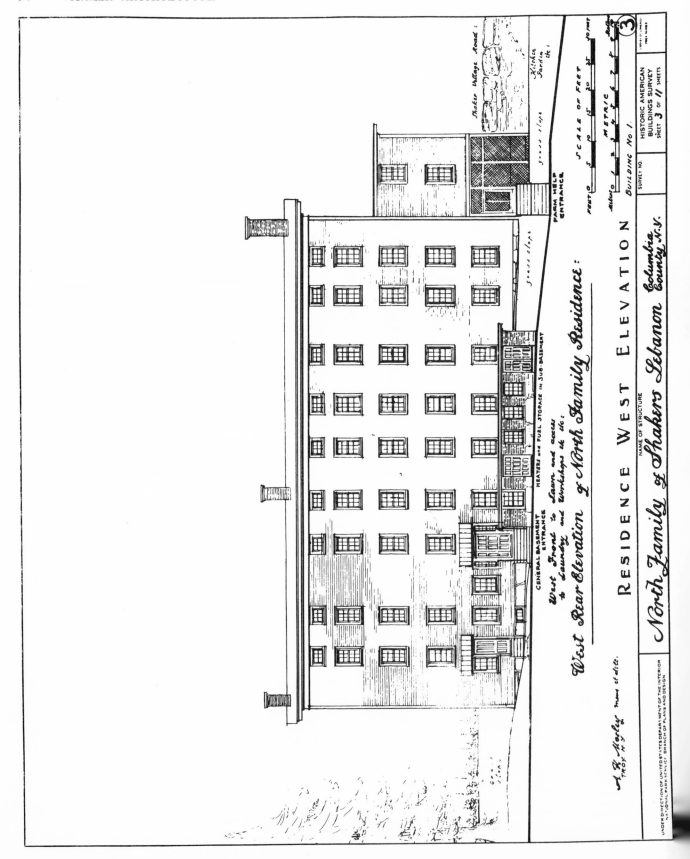

RESIDENCE WEST ELEVATION

West Rear Elevation of North Family Residence:

North Family of Shakers Lebanon Columbia County N.Y.

First Floor Plan:
SCALE 8 FEET to 1 INCH:

MAIN RESIDENCE
PLAN OF FIRST FLOOR
NAME OF STRUCTURE AND LOCATION

North Family of Shakers Lebanon Columbia County N.Y.

BUILDING No. 1.

HISTORIC BUILDINGS SURVEY
SHEET 4 of 11 SHEETS

NEW YORK STATE MUSEUM
HISTORIC COLLECTION

MAIN RESIDENCE
FAMILY MEETING ROOM : BUILDING No. 1

*North Family of Shakers Lebanon Columbia County, N.Y.*

EAST WALL

NORTH WALL

SOUTH WALL

WEST WALL

Closets and Doors

A. K. Mosley MAY 11 1939
TROY. N.Y.

NEW YORK STATE MUSEUM
HIST. PIC. COLLECTION

NAME OF STRUCTURE AND LOCATION

HISTORIC BUILDINGS SURVEY

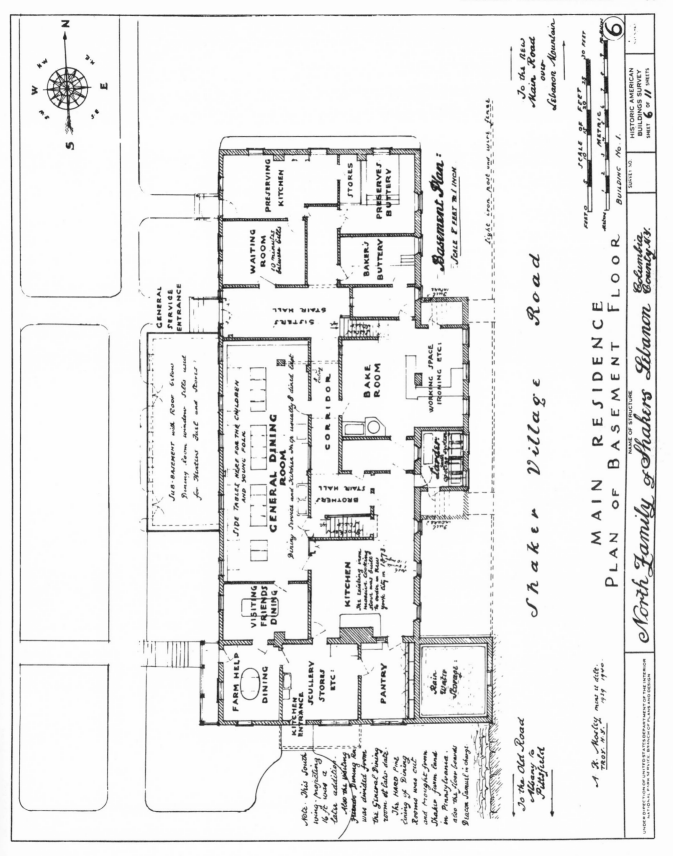

N

GENERAL SERVICE ENTRANCE

PRESERVING KITCHEN

WAITING ROOM
10 minutes between bells

STORES

BAKERS BUTTERY

PRESERVES BUTTERY

SISTERS STAIR HALL

BAKE ROOM

CORRIDOR

WORKING SPACE IRONING ETC.

BROTHERS STAIR HALL

SUB-BASEMENT with Room below

Dining Room window Sills will for Heating Fuel and Stores.

SIDE TABLES HERE FOR THE CHILDREN AND YOUNG FOLK

GENERAL DINING ROOM

Dining Service and Kitchen shop usually 8 dried Click

VISITING FRIENDS DINING

KITCHEN

This building item tremovich Cooking stove was built to order in New York City in 1873.

FARM HELP DINING

KITCHEN ENTRANCE

SCULLERY STORES ETC.

PANTRY

Rain Water Except

Basement Plan:
SCALE 8 FEET TO 1 INCH

Light Iron foot and wire first

Shaker Village Road

MAIN RESIDENCE
PLAN OF BASEMENT FLOOR

North Family of Shakers Lebanon Columbia County N.Y.

NAME OF STRUCTURE

UNDER DIRECTION OF UNITED STATES DEPARTMENT OF THE INTERIOR
NATIONAL PARK SERVICE. BRANCH OF PLANS AND DESIGN

A. R. Morley mwz st diet.
Troy. N.Y. 1939-1940

SURVEY NO.

HISTORIC AMERICAN BUILDINGS SURVEY
SHEET 6 OF 11 SHEETS

BUILDING No. 1.

SCALE OF FEET
FEET 5 0 5 10 20 30 FEET
METRIC

6

To the New Main Road over Lebanon Mountain

To the Old Road Albany to Pittsfield

Note: This South wing projecting 16 ft was a later addition. Also this yielding Friends Dining Room was divided from the General Dining room at later date. This Hard Pine lining of Dining Rooms was cut and wrought from Shaker farm land in Pennsylvania. also this floor boards Deacon Samuel in charge.

Detail of Typical Splay Window Jamb:

Second Floor Plan:

NOTE THE THIRD FLOOR IS SIMILAR TO THE SECOND FLOOR EXCEPT THE SOUTH PROJECTING ROOM IS OMITTED AND THE CENTER CORRIDOR IS CLOSED AT EACH END AND IS USED AS A STORAGE CLOSET.

SISTER MURELLA GALLUP

SISTERS' ROOM

SISTERS' STAIR HALL

ELDER BROTHERS ROOM

ELDRESS ELLA WINSHIP

BROTHERS STAIR HALL

BROTHERS ROOM

BROTHERS ROOM

BROTHERS ROOM

Roof

Shaker Village Road:

MAIN RESIDENCE
PLAN OF SECOND FLOOR

North Family of Shakers Lebanon Columbia County N.Y.

SCALE OF FEET

Internal Vertical Section
SKETCHES TO INDICATE TYPICAL WINDOW TRIM FINISH

HEAD

SILL

HISTORIC AMERICAN BUILDINGS SURVEY
SHEET 7 OF 11 SHEETS

7

Door Jamb

Door Trim

Top

Door Top Rail

(B) 35'8"

Full size details No. 3 Scale:

FLOOR

PLASTER

Attic Window Jambs

ROOF PURLIN cased as CORNICE

BEARING PARTITION TRUSSED:

STORE ROOMS

MAIN ATTIC

Plaster Ceiling

SCALES

HISTORIC AMERICAN BUILDINGS SURVEY
SHEET 8 OF 11 SHEETS

SURVEY NO.

BUILDING No. 1.

No. 1.

Linen Cupboard Front

PLAN OF ATTIC FLOOR
Scale No. 1.

ROOF OVERHANG

LINEN

LINEN CABINET

A T T I C
ALL PLASTERED

Attic Store Rooms used for hanging from low ceiling:

NOTE: THIS ATTIC USED TO STORE SUMMER OR WINTER CLOTHING OF ABOUT 60 INMATES.

Attic Store Rooms used for hanging from low ceiling:

SKELETON SKETCH OF TRUSSED ROOF PURLIN IN PARTITION:

Drawer plan

Drawer Section

Elevation
Section

TYPICAL HOUSEHOLD LINEN CABINETS IN ATTIC:

PLAN OF ATTIC FLOOR
MAIN RESIDENCE: ATTIC FLOOR

North Family of Shakers Lebanon Columbia County N.Y.

UNDER DIRECTION OF UNITED STATES DEPARTMENT OF THE INTERIOR
NATIONAL PARK SERVICE BRANCH OF PLANS AND DESIGN

DETAILS of ORIGINAL STEAM RADIATORS

North Family of the Lebanon Shakers, Columbia County, N.Y.

SOUTH WALL

ELEVATION EAST WALL

NORTH WALL

WEST WALL
ELEVATION:

PLAN of
BASEMENT LARDER
COOLING ROOM :

This Cooling System is furnished by a continuous supply of running cold water - brought down from the Reservoir two miles up Lebanon Mountain with lead pipe laid underground.

The Basement Larder is piped with Inch iron pipe circulating 7 times flow and return around the room. The waste is set to drip into the two shallow water Tanks. In this water are placed stone ware crocks for Butter Milk Cream etc. This meat hanging vegetables etc are stored on slat-wood shelves over.

The original installation about 1875 was by Robbins & Cantwell, Pittsfield Mass.

SKETCH of ORIGINAL COOLING SYSTEM
IN BASEMENT LARDER - NORTH FAMILY :

North Family of the Lebanon Shakers
Columbia County, N.Y.

BUILT 182

SURVEY NO.

HISTORIC AMERICAN BUILDINGS SURVEY
SHEET 10 of 11 SHEETS

INDEX NO. 10

BUILDING No. 1.

A.K. Mosley, mns it del.
TROY, N.Y.

U.S. DEPARTMENT OF THE INTERIOR
OFFICE OF NATIONAL PARKS, BUILDINGS, AND RESERVATIONS
BRANCH OF PLANS AND DESIGN

SKETCH OF BROTHERS' DOORWAY:
A TYPICAL SHAKER ENTRANCE:

SCHEDULE
OF
DRAWINGS

1 Front Elevation facing Shaker Village Rd.
2 North and South Ends
3 West Elevation
4 First Floor Plan
5 Meeting Rm. details
6 Basement Plan
  Dining Room
7 Second and Third Floors
8 Attic and Storage
9 Original Steam Radiation
10 Original Refrigeration
11 Section with Typical Shaker Entrance Door
  SCHEDULE of DRAWINGS

SCALES
No.1 - 1/8 inch = 1 Foot

CROSS SECTION thru' CENTRE
(looking North)

TYPICAL SASH
2'-8" x 5'-0" opening

EXTERNAL WALL FACE
CLAP-BOARDED
4 TO 5 INCH EXPOSURE

DETAIL OF TYPICAL
WINDOW TRIM IN and OUT:
Scale No. 2

EXTERNAL SECTION

INTERNAL SECTION

MAIN RESIDENCE
CROSS SECTION and TYPICAL DETAILS

North Family of Shakers Lebanon County N.Y.
Columbia

NAME OF STRUCTURE AND LOCATION
BUILDING No. 1.
HISTORIC BUILDINGS SURVEY
SHEET 11 OF 11 SHEETS

NEW YORK STATE MUSEUM
HISTORIC COLLECTION

## LAUNDRY BUILDING: NORTH FAMILY, MOUNT LEBANON, NEW YORK

The exterior of this building, as with all other Shaker buildings, is plain and unadorned. The plastered cavetto coves, not uncommon to Shaker buildings, were designed to cut down the escape of heat through the attic during the winter months.

The basement of this building is on the ground level at the west elevation. On the south end is the laundry room; it was well equipped with washing machines, stone washtubs, draining trays, and arch kettles for heating water and scalding laundry.

On the first floor, east entrance, is the large ironing room with sliding clothes racks that were shoved into a special heated compartment for drying laundry during winter months. On the north end are the woodshed and tool repair rooms.

*Laundry Building*

On the second floor, special rooms were assigned to the seed industry, for storage, and carpet-weaving.

In one of the rooms on the second floor, west side, are the perforated zinc pans for drying fruits and vegetables. These "dry kilns" are installed over hot air conduits which branch off the jacket around the furnace in the basement.

The attic was used for drying seeds, herbs, and the laundry, during the winter months. This building was erected in 1854.

General Details.

PLASTER COVE
TO MAIN EAVES CORNICE

SECTION OF HOOD
SHELTER OVER DOORS

REFLECTED
PLAN or SOFFITS
TO DOOR HOOD & EAVES

NORTH
BASEMENT
ENTRANCE

NORTH ELEVATION

EAST ELEVATION

SCALES FOR DETAILS

NORTH AND EAST ELEVATIONS OF LAUNDRY

Woodstore & Laundry — North Family of Shakers — Lebanon
Columbia County, N.Y.

HISTORIC AMERICAN
BUILDINGS SURVEY

FIREWOOD STORE
VENTILATING
LUFFER BOARDS
No 3 scale.

DOOR
IN CENTER OF
WEST FRONT
No 2 scale.

SLIDING DOOR
FIREWOOD STORE
EAST FRONT
No 1 scale.

SOUTH ELEVATION

WEST ELEVATION

WEST AND SOUTH ELEVATIONS OF LAUNDRY

Woodstore &
Laundry North Family of Shakers Lebanon
Columbia County N.Y.

SURVEY NO.

HISTORIC AMERICAN
BUILDINGS SURVEY
SHEET 2 OF 5 SHEETS

UNDER DIRECTION OF UNITED STATES DEPARTMENT OF THE INTERIOR
NATIONAL PARK SERVICE, BRANCH OF PLANS AND DESIGN

FIRST & BASEMENT FLOOR PLANS ETC OF LAUNDRY

Woodstore & North Family of Shakers Lebanon
Laundry Columbia County N.Y.

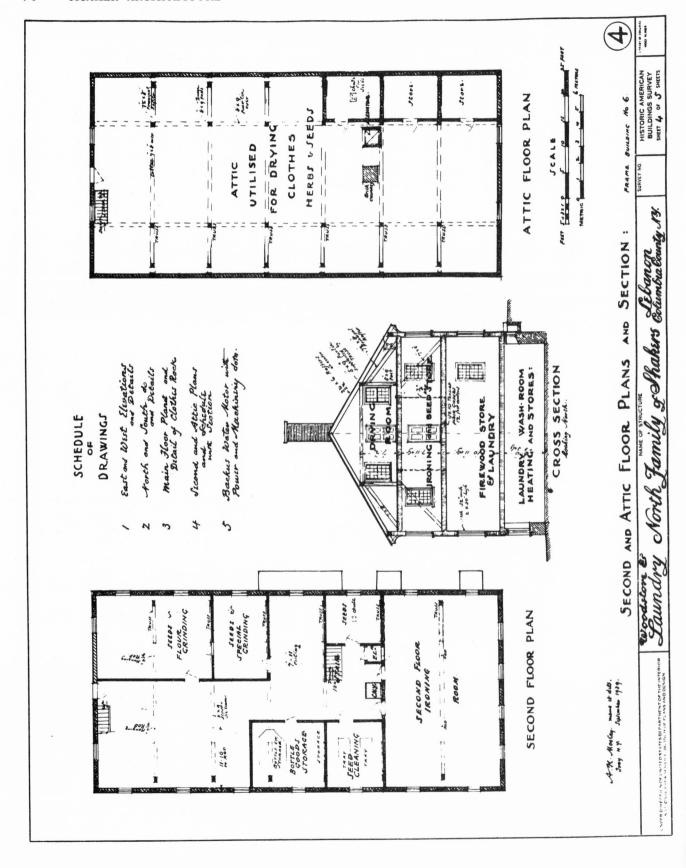

ATTIC FLOOR PLAN

ATTIC UTILISED FOR DRYING CLOTHES HERBS & SEEDS

SCALE

SCHEDULE OF DRAWINGS

1  East and West Elevations and Details
2  North and South Elevations and Details
3  Main Floor Plan and Detail of Clothes Rack
4  Second and Attic Plans and Schedule with Section
5  Backus Water Motor with Power and Machinery data.

CROSS SECTION Looking North.

DRYING ROOM
SEED & LOFT
IRONING
FIREWOOD STORE & LAUNDRY
LAUNDRY WASH-ROOM HEATING, AND STORES.

SECOND FLOOR PLAN

SEEDS FLOUR GRINDING
SEEDS SPECIAL GRINDING
SEEDS
BOTTLE GOODS STORAGE
TRAY SEED CLEANING
STORAGE
SECOND FLOOR IRONING ROOM

SECOND AND ATTIC FLOOR PLANS AND SECTION:

Woolston & Laundry North Family of Shakers Lebanon Columbia County N.Y.

SURVEY NO.  FRANK BUILDING No 6.

HISTORIC AMERICAN BUILDINGS SURVEY
SHEET 4 OF 5 SHEETS

*Sister Folding Towels*

*LUMBER AND GRIST MILL: NORTH FAMILY,
MOUNT LEBANON, NEW YORK*

The Mount Lebanon mill was erected in 1828. Water from a nearby pond on the Church Family property furnished water power for this mill and the "brethren's brick shop."

This· building was demolished in September 1940.

*Lumber and Grist Mill*

PLAN OF MAIN FLOOR:

OPERATED BY WATER-POWER.

LUMBER AND GRIST MILL

North Family, Shakers Lebanon Columbia County N.Y.

NAME OF STRUCTURE AND LOCATION

HISTORIC BUILDINGS SURVEY
SHEET 1 OF 4 SHEETS
BUILDING No. 20 M.F

A.R. McNitty. delt.
TROY N.Y. OCT 1940

NEW YORK STATE MUSEUM
HISTORIC COLLECTION

SCALE OF FEET

HAY MOW.

HAY MOW.

OPEN SPACE

COVERED DRIVEWAY

PARTIALLY COVERED BRIDGE:

STORE

HEAVY GRIST

GRINDING MILL

MILL

PLANING

SAW

HEAVY LUMBER

COVERED SHELTER: OPEN ON THREE SIDES:

LOW-BUILT CAR FOR ROUGH LOGS RUNNING ON METAL RAILS

W = WINDOW !

ENTRANCE FROM THE ALBANY-PITTSFIELD OLD ROAD:

DRIVEWAY RAMP DOWN INTO BASEMENT:

ORIGINAL NATURAL WATER COURSE
FILLED OVER ROUGH STONE
CULVERT

ACCESS TO FIELDS AND WOODS

ABOUT 30 FEET CLEAR JACK
BETWEEN STONE
WALL OF MILL POND
AND MILL BUILDING

POLLED WILLOWS
NOW UP TO 25 FEET
IN DIAMETER !

NOTCH TO PURLIN

OUTER FACE

Details of Typical method of Framing and notching into Purlins or Plates for Roof Rafters.

Purlin at P notched for Roof Rafters, Ears Plate also notched the same!

Sketch of Purlin Queen Post Collar & Principal Rafter.

NOTCH TO PURLIN

INNER FACE

CROSS SECTION SHOWING CONSTRUCTION of EAST GABLE, ETC!

LONGITUDINAL SKELETON SECTION showing FRAMING:

THIS TRUSSED GIRDER FULL LENGTH OF FRONT OF MILL IN ONE UNIT.

SCALES: for DRAWING:

HISTORIC BUILDINGS SURVEY

OPERATED BY WATER POWER:

LUMBER AND GRIST MILL

NAME OF STRUCTURE AND LOCATION

North Family of Shakers Lebanon Columbia County N.Y.

BUILDING

NEW YORK STATE MUSEUM
HISTORIC COLLECTION

PART CROSS SECTION — THROUGH MILL: (showing CENTER ROOF TRUSS)

MAIN FLOOR:

SECOND FLOOR

Details of Special Truss Tie Rods to re-inforce the Center Roof Truss!

8×8 PURLIN IN ONE LENGTH RIGHT THROUGH WITH 3 TRUSS INTERMEDIATE SUPPORTS!

8×8 QUEEN

*A Shaker Carpenter*

### BRETHREN'S RED BRICK SHOP: NORTH FAMILY, MOUNT LEBANON, NEW YORK

A three-story red brick building, with attic and basement, was erected in 1825. Windows were formed of flat gauged brick arches and sills of sawed Stockbridge marble. The basement walls are made of the same sawed marble.

Originally this was the laundry building, but in later years it was known as the "Brethren's Red Brick Shop." This building accommodated the shoemaker's shop, the broom shop, carpenters' shops, and seed shops.

*Brethren's Red Brick Shop*

The large power wheel in the basement was propelled by water from the same stream that turned the lumber and grist mill power wheels.

According to the Millennial Law, Sev. V, Art 23: "Brethren's and sisters' shops should not be under one and the same roof, except those of the Ministry."

©Kermes '61

*In the Shoemaker's Shop*

FIRST FLOOR PLAN:

TOTAL 42'·7"

40'·5¾"

25'·10"

10'·0"

ENTRANCE HALL and STAIR LANDING
MAIN FLOOR

Stair Treads
Risers
8' wide
on Plan

TOTAL 64'·3"

25'·2"

SECOND FLOOR PLAN

STAIR LANDING
SECOND FLOOR

Note: All ordinary window openings are 3'·2" wide and 5'·7½" high, in each opening

EAST ELEVATION AT THE BEND OF SHAKER VILLAGE ROAD

SCALE of FEET

METRIC

HISTORIC BUILDINGS SURVEY
SHEET 1 of 8 SHEETS

BUILDING No. 18

NORTH ELEVATION TO SHAKER VILLAGE ROAD:

OPEN AIR BRIDGE

ELEVATIONS WITH FIRST AND SECOND FLOOR PLANS:

NAME OF STRUCTURE AND LOCATION

Original Laundry North Family of Shakers Lebanon
& Watervliet Building Columbia County N.Y.

NEW YORK STATE MUSEUM
HISTORIC COLLECTION

A.K. Morley, New York delt
Troy N.Y. November 1940

EAVES

RAKING

HALF GABLE

HORIZONTAL

PROFILE DETAILS OF
TYPICAL SHELTER HOOD OVER-
SHAKER ENTRANCE DOOR WAYS
Scale No 1 3 inches to 1 foot

PLASTER
COVE &
CORNICE
AT EAVES
Scale No 2
3 inches
equals 1 foot

SAWN MARBLE
BASE AT
MAIN FLOOR
Scale No 3
Six inches
equals one foot

MUNTON (M)
Scale No 3
equals one foot

NORTH AND SOUTH
DOORS
Scale No 4
Half inch to 1 foot

3'·11"

6'·9"
8'·0"

LONGITUDINAL SECTION:

CROSS SECTION:

Scale:
No 1 SCALE OF FEET

SECTIONS AND DETAILS:

NAME OF STRUCTURE AND LOCATION

Original Laundry,
& Waterwheel Building North Family of Shakers Columbia County N.Y. Lebanon

BUILDING
No. 18

NEW YORK STATE MUSEUM
HISTORIC COLLECTION

HISTORIC BUILDINGS SURVEY
SHEET 3 OF 8

MILL POND 22

Schedule of Drawings

ORIGINAL LAUNDRY and FRAME SMITHY.
BUILDINGS 18 and 19 NORTH FAMILY

1 First and Second Floors & 2 Elevations
2 Attic and Third Floors - & 2 Elevation
3 Two Sections and details
4 Basement and Smithy with schedule of drawings
5 Trip Hammer Air-supply & Smithy Fires
6 Ox Shoeing Frame Perspective Sketch
7 Do    do    do    Assembly details
8 Do    do    do    do

FRAME BUILDING No 19 ABOUT 21 x 60 used as SMITHY by the NORTH FAMILY

Building used for Storage of Mechanical parts - Metal Hardware.

Smithy Entrance

BRIDGE OVERHEAD

Note. FRAME BUILDING 19. NORTH FAMILY SMITHY No 19 on Village Map. used for Several Smiths work and Horse and Cattle Shoeing and Storage of Hardware, Metal patterns, Wagon and Carry-off etc. Site also repairs drawings of Smith Forge with Bellows, Ox Trip Hammer, and Ox shoeing Cradle Water Power was made available from Building 18.

RECEIVING AND DISPATCHING GOODS

WATER WHEEL PIT

NOTE. THIS HEAVY STONE WALLING HAS EVIDENTLY SUPPORTED AN ORIGINAL WATER WHEEL - IN THE OPEN AIR - OVERSHOT TYPE. SUBSEQUENTLY A NEW BUILDING IS BUILT CONTAINING A WATER WHEEL PIT WITHIN THE BASEMENT : ALSO AT THE SAME TIME GIVING 8 or 10 FEET MORE HEAD!

GROUND FLOOR PLAN : Building No. 18.

Original Laundry & Waterwheel Building North Family of Shakers Lebanon Columbia County N.Y.

NAME OF STRUCTURE AND LOCATION

NEW YORK STATE MUSEUM HISTORIC COLLECTION

HISTORIC BUILDINGS SURVEY SHEET 4 of 8 SHEETS

SCALE OF FEET

4

## MEETING HOUSE: CHURCH FAMILY, MOUNT LEBANON, NEW YORK

This meeting house was erected in 1824 entirely by the brethren of Lebanon; Watervliet, New York; Enfield, New Hampshire and Shirley, Massachusetts, and other Shaker communities. The total cost was estimated by Brother Alonzo Hollister to have been more than $16,000. Of this amount, the Shakers of Canterbury and Enfield, New Hampshire, contributed $500, and the Societies at Enfield, Connecticut, and Hancock, Massachusetts, donated $600. The Church Family of the Harvard, Massachusetts, Society furnished the glass for the windows. The Shirley, Massachusetts, Society donated the services of Brother Jonas Nutting from July 12 to September 15, 1824.

*Meeting House*

This is one of the most interesting buildings to be found in any Shaker community. The barrel, or rainbow roof, planned to shed snow, and its intricate supporting frame work are worthy of special study. The Meeting Room, sixty-three feet by seventy-eight feet four inches, has no interior suuports. The two chimneys (north and south walls) were designed for the four large cast-iron stoves that heated the auditorium or "Meeting Room." These stoves are now in the Shaker Museum, Old Chatham, New York.

The wing on the south side housed members of the Ministry, elders, and eldresses. It provided work rooms as well as retiring rooms for them.

The entrance doorway to this wing embodies another beautiful architectural detail in Shaker buildings, but certainly unintentional, because the Millennial Laws constantly forbade planned beauty. The combination of rightness cf line and proportion achieved a work of art in this detail.

"The Meeting House should be painted white without and of a bluish shade within. . . . No building may be white save meeting houses." Millennial Law, Sec. I, Arts. 3 and 6.

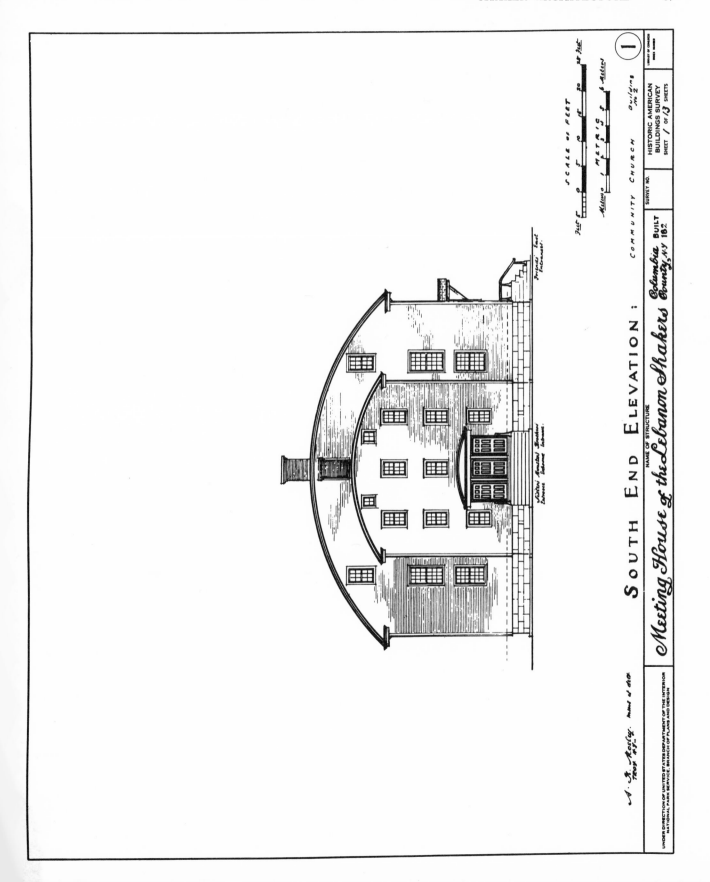

SOUTH END ELEVATION:

SCALE OF FEET

METRIS

COMMUNITY CHURCH        Building No 2

A. R. Mosley. Head of dep
Troy N.Y.

Meeting House of the Lebanon Shakers Columbia
County, N.Y. 182.

NAME OF STRUCTURE

SURVEY NO. 162        HISTORIC AMERICAN
BUILDINGS SURVEY
SHEET 1 OF 13 SHEETS

UNDER DIRECTION OF UNITED STATES DEPARTMENT OF THE INTERIOR
NATIONAL PARK SERVICE, BRANCH OF PLANS AND DESIGN

East Side Elevation:

Meeting House of the Lebanon Shakers

COMMUNITY CHURCH

Columbia County, N.Y.

BUILT 182

SURVEY NO.

HISTORIC AMERICAN BUILDINGS SURVEY
SHEET 2 OF 13 SHEETS

INDEX NO. 2

NAME OF STRUCTURE

U.S. DEPARTMENT OF THE INTERIOR
OFFICE OF NATIONAL PARKS, BUILDINGS, AND RESERVATIONS
BRANCH OF PLANS AND DESIGN

SCALE OF FEET

METRIC

BUILDING NO. 2.

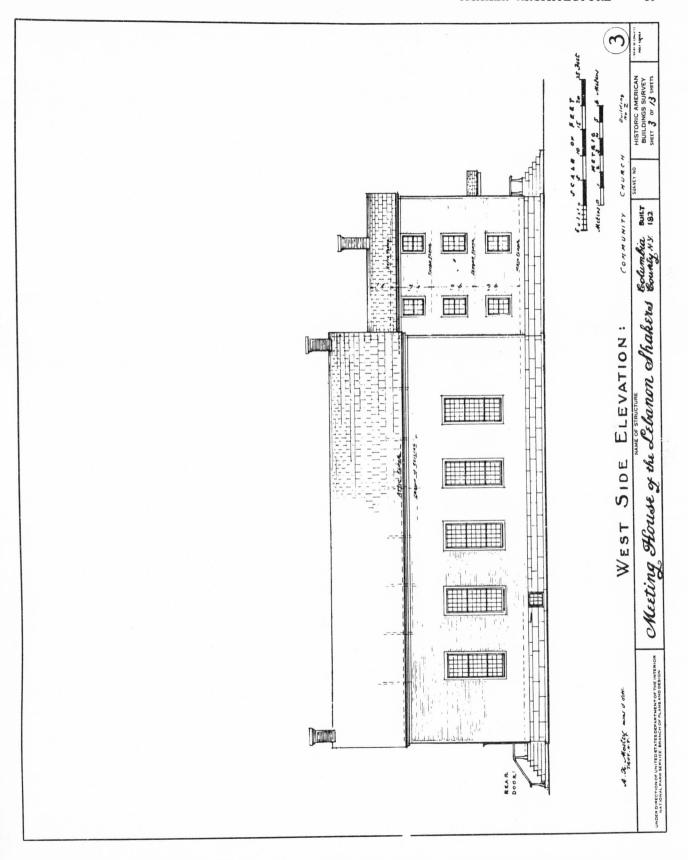

WEST SIDE ELEVATION:

*Meeting House of the Lebanon Shakers*

COMMUNITY CHURCH

NAME OF STRUCTURE

Columbia County, N.Y.

BUILT 182

SURVEY NO

Building No 2

HISTORIC AMERICAN
BUILDINGS SURVEY
SHEET 3 OF 13 SHEETS

SCALE OF FEET

METERS

REAR DOOR

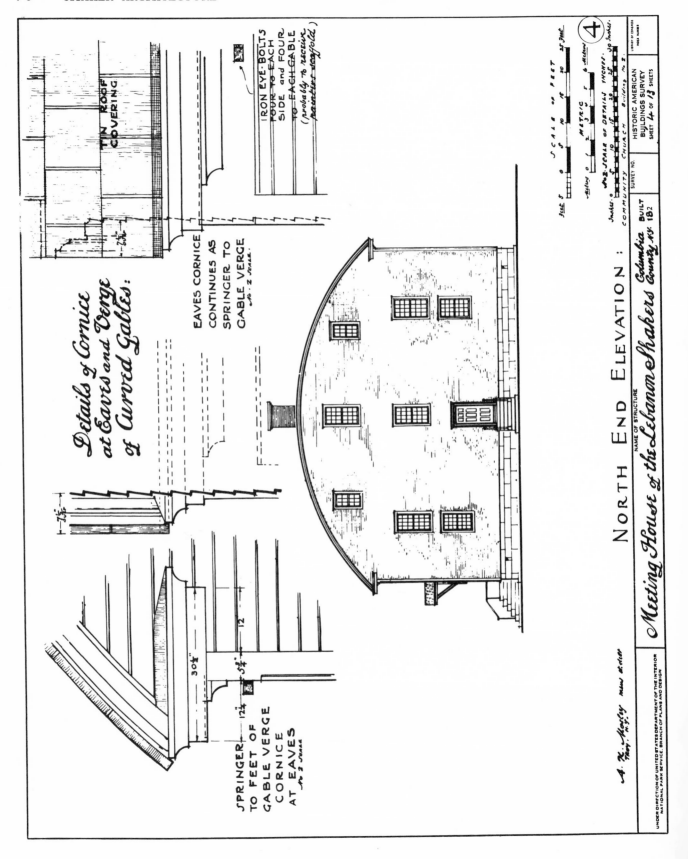

TIN ROOF COVERING

IRON EYE-BOLTS FOUR TO EACH SIDE and FOUR TO EACH GABLE (probably to receive painters scaffold)

Details of Cornice at Eaves and Verge of Curved Gables:

EAVES CORNICE CONTINUES AS SPRINGER TO GABLE VERGE
Nº 2 SCALE

SPRINGER TO FEET OF GABLE VERGE CORNICE AT EAVES
Nº 3 SCALE

30¼"
12
5¼"
12¼

NORTH END ELEVATION:

Meeting House of the Lebanon Shakers Columbia County, N.Y.

NAME OF STRUCTURE

A. K. Hosley meas. & drew
Troy, N.Y.

UNDER DIRECTION OF UNITED STATES DEPARTMENT OF THE INTERIOR
NATIONAL PARK SERVICE, BRANCH OF PLANS AND DESIGN

COMMUNITY CHURCH Building Nº 2

BUILT 1B2

HISTORIC AMERICAN BUILDINGS SURVEY
SHEET 4 of 13 SHEETS

SURVEY NO.

LIBRARY OF CONGRESS FILE NUMBER

SCALE OF FEET

Nº 2 SCALE OF DETAILS INCHES
METRIC

Wagon Sheds mostly for the Canaan and East (Hill) and South Shaker Families

This North Door used mostly by Drunks & Wagons bringing the Outside Families to Meeting

65.6 outside wood

65.3¾ outside Base

63.4½ inside

80.8 outside Base 80.8 outside wood

79.4½ inside

TEMPORARY PLATFORM (MODERN)

M E E T I N G

R O O M

etc.

OF THE

LEBANON SHAKER COMMUNITY

63.4" × 78.4"

FRIENDS & VISITORS BALCONY OCCUPIED BY WOMEN VISITORS BALCONY

FRONT ROW OCCUPIED BY SHAKER CHILDREN

FRIENDS & MEN VISITORS BALCONY

WOMEN VISITING FRIENDS

WOMEN

SIDE ENTRANCE:

WOMEN VISITING FRIENDS

80.8 outside

MEN

SIDE ENTRANCE:

MEN VISITING FRIENDS

15.7½

15.7½

27.6½

SISTERS' ENTRANCE AND CLOAK ROOM:

BROTHERS ENTRANCE AND COAT ROOM:

SISTERS
MINISTERS
BROTHERS

31.5 front

MAIN ENTRANCE

See separate plans of newer Ministers Residence in later years located here. (about 1890)

OF MINISTERS RESIDENCE

PAVED WALK TO FRONT ENTRANCE

PAVED SIDEWALK

West Side of the Shaker Village Road

PAVED SIDE WALK

N
W E
S

FIRST FLOOR PLAN

Meeting House of the Lebanon Shakers

NAME OF STRUCTURE

Columbia County N.Y.

SURVEY NO.

BUILT 1821

SIDE WALK PAVED WITH SELF-FACED STONE ALONG WEST SIDE SHAKER VILLAGE ROAD

COMMUNITY CHURCH Building No. 2

SCALE OF FEET
feet 0 5 10 15 20 feet
METRES
metres 1 0 1 2 3 metres

HISTORIC AMERICAN BUILDINGS SURVEY
SHEET 5 OF 13 SHEETS

5

LIBRARY OF CONGRESS
FILE NUMBER

UNDER DIRECTION OF UNITED STATES DEPARTMENT OF THE INTERIOR
NATIONAL PARK SERVICE, BRANCH OF PLANS AND DESIGN

A. H. Mosley, delin.
May 1939 tracing.

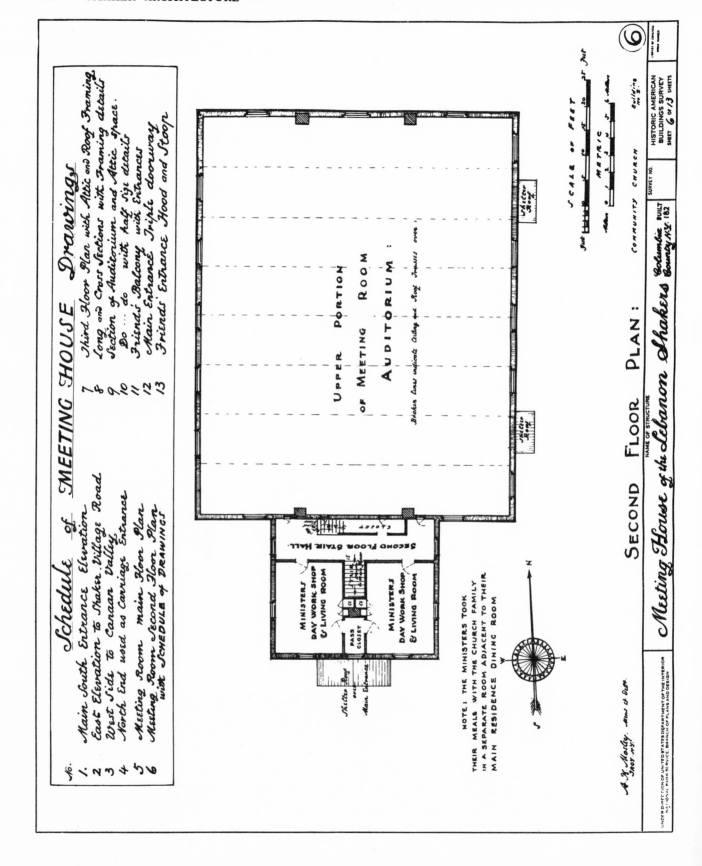

## Schedule of MEETING HOUSE Drawings

No.
1. Main South Entrance Elevation
2. East Elevation to Shaker Village Road
3. West Side to Canaan Valley
4. North End used as Carriage Entrance
5. Meeting Room main Floor Plan
6. Meeting Room Second Floor Plan with SCHEDULE of DRAWINGS
7. Third Floor Plan with Attic and Roof Framing
8. Long and Cross Sections with framing details
9. Section of Auditorium and Attic Space
10. Do ...do with half size details
11. Friends Balcony with Entrance
12. Main Entrance Triple doorway
13. Friends Entrance Hood and Stoop

### UPPER PORTION of MEETING ROOM AUDITORIUM:

Broken lines indicate Ceiling and Roof Trusses over

SECOND FLOOR STAIR HALL

CLOSET

MINISTERS DAY WORK SHOP & LIVING ROOM

MINISTERS DAY WORK SHOP & LIVING ROOM

PASS CLOSET

Main Entrance

NOTE: THE MINISTERS TOOK THEIR MEALS WITH THE CHURCH FAMILY IN A SEPARATE ROOM ADJACENT TO THEIR MAIN RESIDENCE DINING ROOM

## SECOND FLOOR PLAN:

Meeting House of the Lebanon Shakers

SCALE OF FEET
METRIC

A. G. Morley, Arch't & Delr.
Troy, N.Y.

UNDER DIRECTION OF UNITED STATES DEPARTMENT OF THE INTERIOR
NATIONAL PARK SERVICE, BRANCH OF PLANS AND DESIGN

BUILT 182

NAME OF STRUCTURE
COMMUNITY CHURCH

Columbia County, N.Y.

SURVEY NO.

HISTORIC AMERICAN BUILDINGS SURVEY
SHEET 6 OF 13 SHEETS

THIRD FLOOR PLAN AND ROOF TRUSSES IN ATTIC OVER AUDITORIUM

*Meeting House of the Lebanon Shakers*

ATTIC OVER PROJECTING FRONT BLOCK - *portion over Attic Landing "plastered"*

HISTORIC AMERICAN BUILDINGS SURVEY
SHEET 7 OF 73 SHEETS

COMMUNITY CHURCH

NAME OF STRUCTURE
Columbia County N.Y.

UNDER DIRECTION OF UNITED STATES DEPARTMENT OF THE INTERIOR
NATIONAL PARK SERVICE BRANCH OF PLANS AND DESIGN

Roof Trusses over Auditorium:

Meeting House of the Lebanon Shakers, Columbia County, N.Y.

NAME OF STRUCTURE AND LOCATION

Community Church Building

HISTORIC BUILDINGS SURVEY

SHEET 8 OF 13 SHEETS

NEW YORK STATE MUSEUM HISTORIC COLLECTION

CROSS SECTION OF AUDITORIUM LOOKING NORTH

Meeting House of the Lebanon Shakers

North Wall of Meeting House Auditorium.

PLASTER WALL AND CHIMNEY.

WALNUT SPANDREL BOARDING

MEETING HOUSE AUDITORIUM FLOOR.

ATTIC BOARD WALK

BRICK SMOKE FLUE. SUPPORTED BY TWO PLANKS EACH 3×10 BRACED AT HEAD

ROOF COVERED WITH SHEET TIN OVER 1¼ T&G ROOF BOARDING ON 3×6 ROOF PURLINS WHICH ARE TENONED INTO THE 10×10 CURVED LAMINATED PRINCIPAL RAFTER OF FOUR 2½×10 PLANKS

10×10 LAMINATED PRINCIPAL RAFTER

3×6 PURLINS

SURVEY NO.
HISTORIC AMERICAN BUILDINGS SURVEY
SHEET 9 OF 13 SHEETS

NAME OF STRUCTURE
COMMUNITY CHURCH
BUILT 1824
Columbia County, N.Y.

UNDER DIRECTION OF UNITED STATES DEPARTMENT OF THE INTERIOR
NATIONAL PARK SERVICE, BRANCH OF PLANS AND DESIGN

General Details of Eaves Cornice, Door and Window Jambs:

MAIN EAVES CORNICE SCALE NO. 2

PLAN OF EYE-BOLT

Cross Section of Auditorium looking SOUTH:

MEETING HOUSE AUDITORIUM LOOKING SOUTH

DETAIL OF TYPICAL SHAKER PEG-RAIL

Meeting House of the Lebanon Shakers, Columbia County, N.Y.

SCALES

NEW YORK STATE MUSEUM HISTORIC COLLECTION

HISTORIC BUILDINGS SURVEY
COMMUNITY CHURCH BUILDING No. 2
SHEET 10 OF 13 SHEETS

SCALE No. 3.
THUMB LATCH

DETAIL B B
supports to Balcony Seating

EXTERNAL

INTERNAL

$1\frac{3}{4} \times 1\frac{3}{4}$ Head rail

SCALE No. 2
DETAIL OF LOWER STEPS of BALCONY

SECTION of BALCONY
(looking North)

SCALES

Sketches of Wrot. Iron door Hardware
Ring grip handles : Thumb latch etc:
SCALE No. 3       ONE-HALF ACTUAL SIZE

INTERNAL

MEETING Ho. AUDITORIUM FLOOR

FRIENDS ENTRANCE DOORS and BALCONYS
Located in East Wall of Meeting House Auditorium
Note. Two exactly similar Doorways and Balconys
The Northernmost for Men, the Southernmost for Women:

EXTERNAL

COUTSIDE FACE of DOOR

INSIDE FACE of DOOR

GRIP RING HANDLES
IN AND OUT TO
FRIENDS DOORS

NEW YORK STATE MUSEUM
HISTORIC COLLECTION

FRIENDS ENTRANCE DOORS and BALCONYS
NAME OF STRUCTURE AND LOCATION

Meeting-House of the Lebanon Shakers Columbia County N.Y.

COMMUNITY CHURCH BUILDING 2.
HISTORIC BUILDINGS SURVEY
SHEET 11 OF 13 SHEETS

PROFILE OF CURVED ROOF VERGE

CURVED ROOF VERGE SOFFITE

PROFILE A

PROFILE OF V

DOOR-JAMB & TRIM AT J

SKETCH OF TRIPLE ENTRANCE DOOR HOOD:

SECTION AT CENTER

ELEVATION TRIPLE DOOR AND HOOD

DETAILS OF MAIN ENTRANCE

PROFILE BB

Meeting House of the Lebanon Shakers

NAME OF STRUCTURE

Columbia County, N.Y.

HISTORIC AMERICAN BUILDINGS SURVEY
SHEET 12 OF 13 SHEETS

Community Church - Building 2.

PROFILE **C** **C** CURVED CORNICE:

SECTION **F** **S** **W** FACE to WALL ACROSS SOFFITE OF HOOD. *scale no 2.*

SECTION OF PROJECTING DOOR HOOD & STEPS

*The pair of Four Piece Reinforcing Brackets are Modern.*

SCALES

*Metric Scale*

EAST ELEVATION of DOORWAY.

TYPICAL DETAIL WOOD RAIL & NEWEL SUPPORT

ELEVATION NORTH SIDE PROJECTING HOOD & STEPS

STONE STEPS

IRON DOWEL

FRIENDS ENTRANCE DOORS—HOOD & STEPS:

*Meeting House of the Lebanon Shakers* Columbia County N.Y.

NAME OF STRUCTURE AND LOCATION

HISTORIC BUILDINGS SURVEY
COMMUNITY CHURCH - BUILDING 2
SHEET 13 OF 13 SHEETS

13

A. H. Mosley Troy, N.Y.

NEW YORK STATE MUSEUM
HISTORIC COLLECTION

*An Entrance to the Meeting House*

### MINISTRY'S DWELLING HOUSE: CHURCH FAMILY, MOUNT LEBANON, NEW YORK

"Odd or fanciful styles of architecture may not be used among the Believers: neither should any deviate widely from the common styles of buildings among Believers, without the Union of the Leaders or Ministry." Millennial Laws, Sec. IX, Art 2.

The above law was broken when this red brick building was erected, for there is a great deviation from the traditional Shaker style of architecture. It has decorative window and door arches, and mouldings and cornices which are far too ornate to pass unnoticed in a Shaker community.

Who was at fault will never be known. Did the Ministry give its consent to these changes, or was it the employed world's laborer who could not

*Ministry's Dwelling House*

get away from the prevailing Victorian influence? There are, however, many Shaker features embodied such as the off-center front doors, cut stone foundation, and other exterior and interior details.

The building was erected for the use of the Ministry at the time of the construction of the Main Dwelling House in 1875. The stone, dated 1841 and imbedded in the foundation of rear of the wing, is from the first Ministry House, one of the eight buildings destroyed by a pyromaniacal hired man on the evening of February 6, 1875.

*Members of the Ministry*

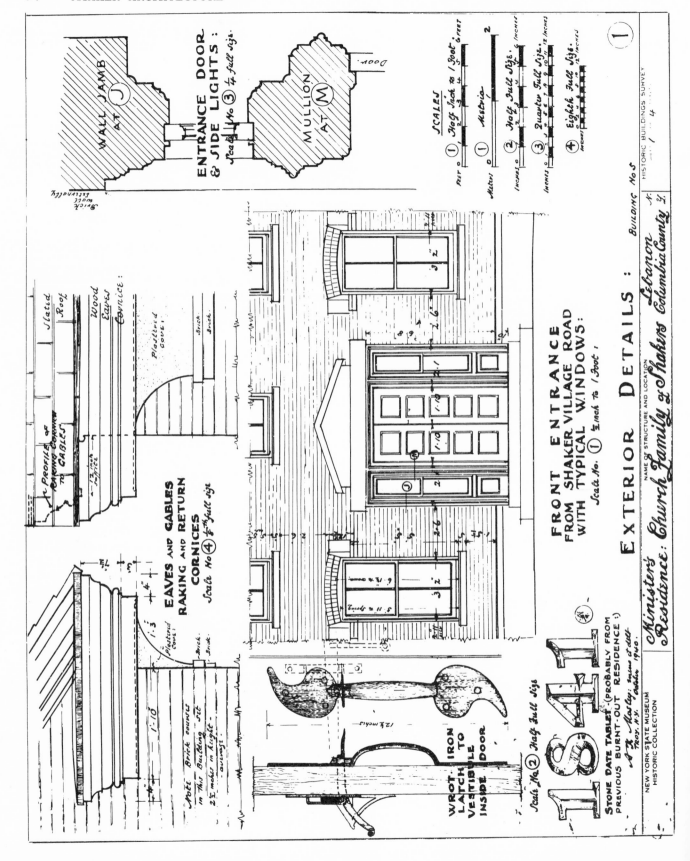

WALL JAMB AT J

ENTRANCE DOOR & SIDE LIGHTS :
Scale No ③ ¼ full size.

MULLION AT M

Door.

Brick wall externally.

SCALES

① Half Inch to 1 Foot :

① Metric:

② Half Full Size.

③ Quarter Full Size.

④ Eighth Full Size.

①

Slated Roof
Wood Eaves
Cornice :

Plastered Cove :

Brick
Brick

PROFILE OF RAKING CORNICE TO GABLES

EAVES AND GABLES
RAKING AND RETURN
CORNICES
Scale No ④ ⅛ full size.

Plastered Cove :
Brick
Brick

Note Brick course in this Building — 2½ inches in height — average.

WROT. IRON LATCH TO VESTIBULE INSIDE DOOR.

12½ inches.

Scale No ② Half Full Size

1841

STONE DATE TABLET : (PROBABLY FROM PREVIOUS BURNT-OUT RESIDENCE :)

FRONT ENTRANCE
FROM SHAKER VILLAGE ROAD
WITH TYPICAL WINDOWS:
Scale No ① ½ inch to 1 foot :

EXTERIOR DETAILS :

Ministers' Residence: Church Family of Shakers of Lebanon Columbia County.

EAST ELEVATION:
FRONT TO SHAKER VILLAGE ROAD

SOUTH ELEVATION:

ELEVATIONS EAST AND SOUTH.

NAME OF STRUCTURE AND LOCATION

Ministers' Residence   Church Family of Shakers   Lebanon Columbia County N.Y.

BUILDING No 5

SCALE OF FEET:

METRIC SCALE of METERS

HISTORIC BUILDINGS SURVEY
SHEET 2 OF 4 SHEETS

2

HISTORIC COLLECTION NO

NEW YORK STATE MUSEUM
HISTORIC COLLECTION

SCHEDULE of MINISTERS' RESIDENCE
DRAWINGS.

1 Front Entrance and details
2 East and South Elevations
3 North and West Elevations
4 First and Second Floor Plans

WEST ELEVATION

NORTH ELEVATION:

ELEVATIONS WEST AND NORTH

Ministers'
Residence: Church Family of Shakers Lebanon Columbia County N.Y.

NEW YORK STATE MUSEUM
HISTORIC COLLECTION

BUILDING No 5

HISTORIC BUILDINGS SURVEY
SHEET 3 OF 4 SHEETS

3

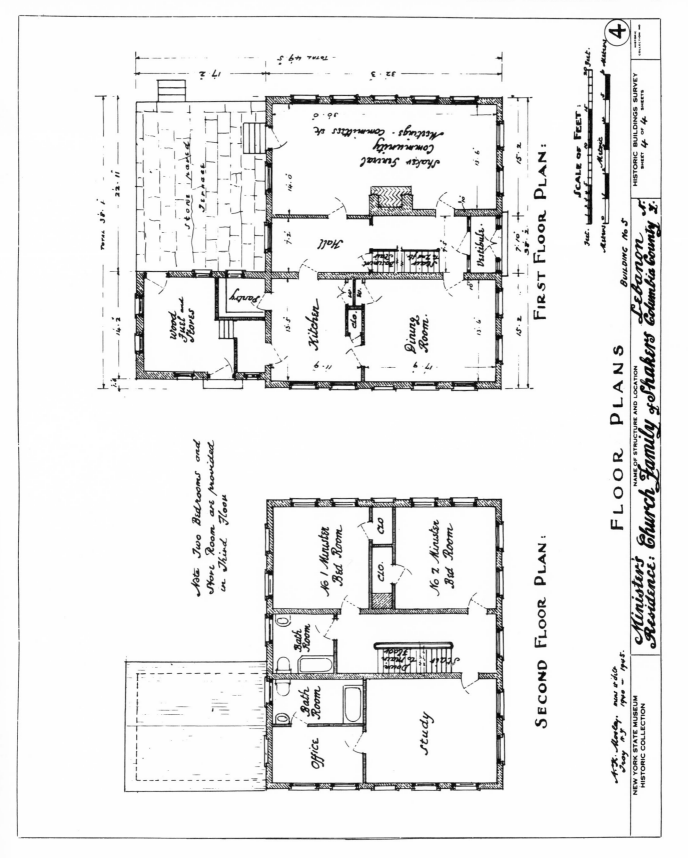

FLOOR PLANS

FIRST FLOOR PLAN:

Shaker Several Community Meetings - Committees etc.

Hall

Vestibule

Wood Shed and Stoves

Pantry

Kitchen

Clo.

Dining Room.

Stone Arches

Furnace

SECOND FLOOR PLAN:

Note: Two Bedrooms and Store Room are provided in Third Floor

No 1 Minister Bed Room

Clo

Clo.

Clo.

No 2 Minister Bed Room

Bath Room

Bath Room

Office

Study

SCALE OF FEET:

Inch:

Metric:

4

HISTORIC BUILDINGS SURVEY
SHEET 4 OF 4 SHEETS

NAME OF STRUCTURE AND LOCATION
BUILDING No 5

Minister's Residence: Church Family of Shakers Lebanon Jr.
Columbia County L.

A.R. Morley, Measured & Delin
Troy N.Y. 1940 - 1945.

NEW YORK STATE MUSEUM
HISTORIC COLLECTION

### BLACKSMITH'S SHOP: CHURCH FAMILY
### MOUNT LEBANON, NEW YORK

This two-story and basement building is of native limestone. It has a plastered roof cove, like that found in many Shaker buildings. The twin chimney flues are unique.

The water-wheel pit measures six feet nine inches wide to eighteen feet deep. It reaches from the subterranean level to the ceiling of the basement.

On the outside wall, over the first floor windows, are cast-iron numerals which give the date of construction as 1846.

*Blacksmith's Shop*

*In the Blacksmith's Shop*

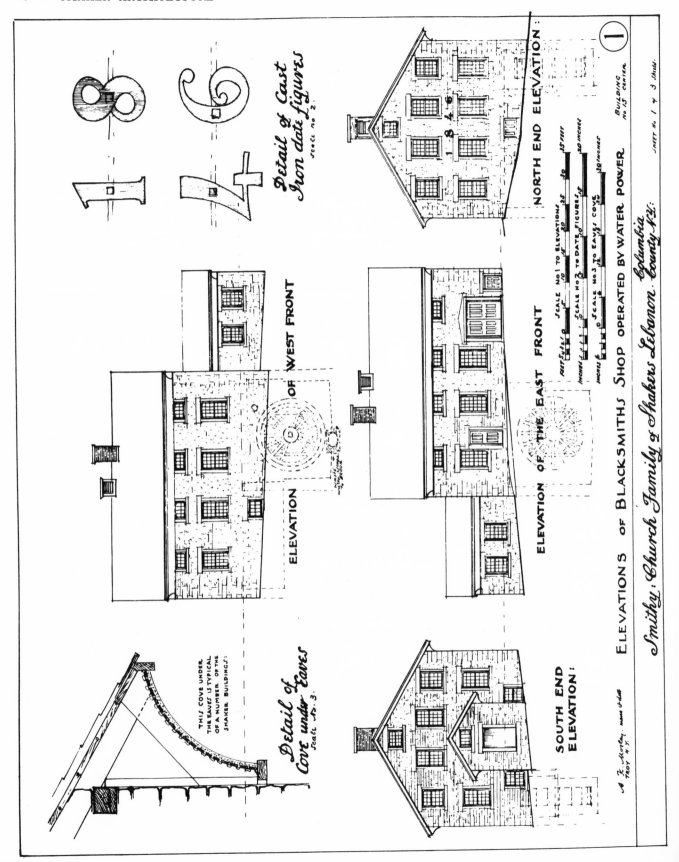

Detail of Cast
Iron date figures
Scale No. 2

NORTH END ELEVATION:

ELEVATION OF WEST FRONT

ELEVATION OF THE EAST FRONT

Detail of
Cove under Eaves
Scale No. 3

THIS COVE UNDER
THE EAVES IS TYPICAL
OF A NUMBER OF THE
SHAKER BUILDINGS:

SOUTH END
ELEVATION:

A. K. Mortee, New York
Troy N.Y.

ELEVATIONS OF BLACKSMITHS SHOP OPERATED BY WATER POWER

BUILDING
No. 15 CENTER

Smithy: Church Family of Shakers Lebanon. Columbia County N.Y.

SHEET No. 1 of 3 SHEETS.

SCALE No. 1 TO ELEVATIONS

SCALE No. 2 TO DATE FIGURES

SCALE No. 3 TO EAVES COVE

BASEMENT PLAN:

WATER-WHEEL PIT: ABOUT 18 ft. CEILING TO FLOOR OF PIT.

SCALE OF FEET

METRIC SCALE

BUILDING No 15 Center.

HISTORIC AMERICAN BUILDINGS SURVEY
SHEET 2 OF 3 SHEETS

SURVEY NO

SMITHY MAIN FLOOR PLAN:

SIDE DOOR

MAIN ENTRANCE DOOR

STAIR

FLOOR PLANS MAIN AND BASEMENT OF BLACKSMITH SHOP OPERATED BY WATER POWER

NAME OF STRUCTURE

Smithy: Church Family of Shakers Lebanon Columbia County N.Y.

A. K. Mosley min. 16 dip. Troy, N.Y.

UNDER DIRECTION OF UNITED STATES DEPARTMENT OF THE INTERIOR
NATIONAL PARK SERVICE, BRANCH OF PLANS AND DESIGN

CROSS SECTION
INDICATING PIT FOR THE
WATER WHEEL IN
SUB-BASEMENT

SMITHY SECOND FLOOR

SECTION AND SECOND FLOOR PLAN OF BLACKSMITH SHOP OPERATED BY WATER POWER :

Smithy: Church Family of Shakers. Lebanon, Columbia County, N.Y.

Sheet No. 3 of 3 sheets

## SHAKER SCHOOL: CHURCH FAMILY, MOUNT LEBANON, NEW YORK

Erected in 1839, this Shaker building at one time served as a school for the six "families," or groups, in the Mount Lebanon Shaker village. From the foundation to the second floor the schoolhouse is made of irregular limestone blocks. It has upper and lower classrooms. The overhanging door canopy of the front entrance is duplicated over the rear door, which is the entrance to second-floor classroom.

*Shaker School*

*The Schoolmaster and His Pupils*

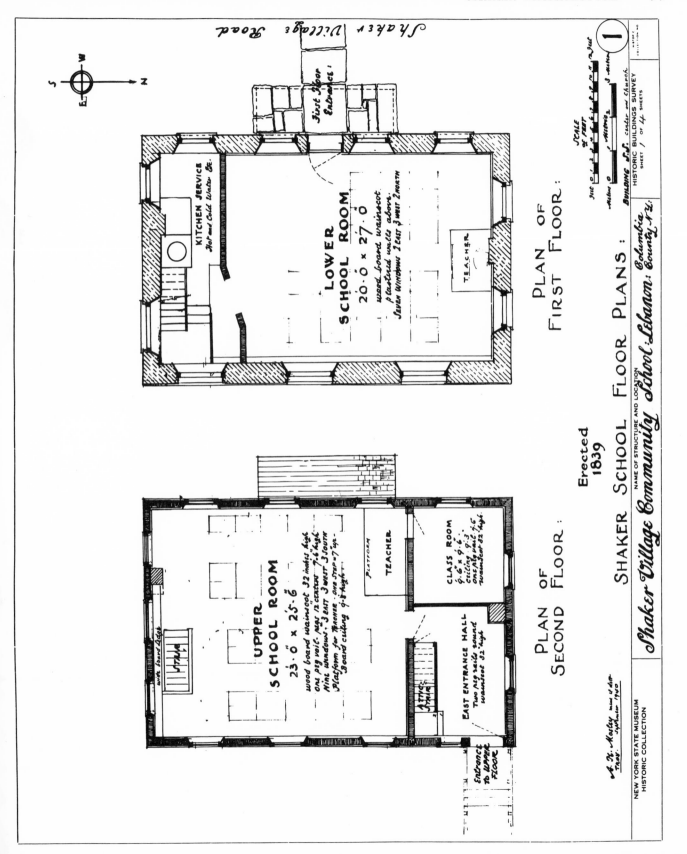

Shaker Village Road

First Floor Entrances

KITCHEN SERVICE
Hot and Cold Water &c.

LOWER
SCHOOL ROOM
20.0 x 27.0
wood board wainscot
plastered walls above.
Seven Windows 2 East 3 West 2 North

TEACHER

PLAN OF
FIRST FLOOR:

Erected
1839

PLAN OF
SECOND FLOOR:

UPPER
SCHOOL ROOM
23.0 x 25.6
wood board wainscot 32 inches high
one ply wall, neat plaster. 7.6 high.
Nine Windows. 3 East 3 West 3 South
Platform for Teacher - one step - 7 ½.
Board ceiling 9.8 high.

STAGE

with board light

PLATFORM

TEACHER

CLASS ROOM
9.6 x 9.6.
ceiling 9.3.
one ply wall 7.6
wainscot 32 high

ATTIC STAIRS

EAST ENTRANCE HALL
Two ply rails sound
wainscot 32 high

Entrance
to UPPER
FLOOR

A. H. Mosley measured
Feb. 1940

SHAKER SCHOOL FLOOR PLANS:

NAME OF STRUCTURE AND LOCATION
Shaker Village Community School: Lebanon: Columbia County, N.Y.

SCALE
¼ = FEET

BUILDING S.J. Cellar and Church
HISTORIC BUILDINGS SURVEY
SHEET 1 OF 4 SHEETS

1

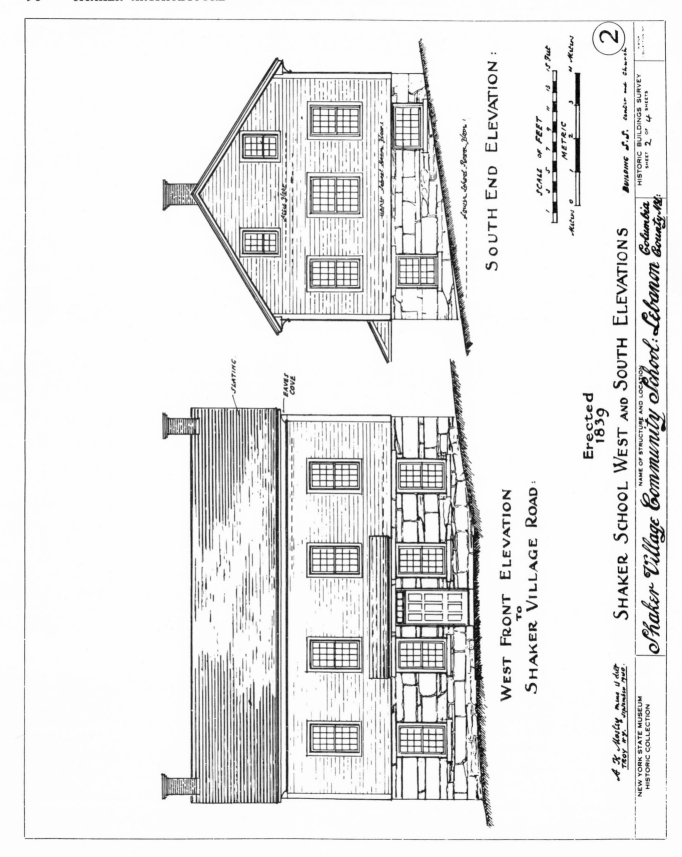

SOUTH END ELEVATION:

WEST FRONT ELEVATION
TO
SHAKER VILLAGE ROAD:

Erected
1839

SHAKER SCHOOL WEST AND SOUTH ELEVATIONS

Shaker Village Community School: Lebanon Columbia County N.Y.

NAME OF STRUCTURE AND LOCATION

BUILDING S.S. Center and Church

HISTORIC BUILDINGS SURVEY
SHEET 2 OF 4 SHEETS

A.Z. Healy meas & delt
Troy N.Y. September 1939

NEW YORK STATE MUSEUM
HISTORIC COLLECTION

SCHEDULE of DRAWINGS

1 Two Floor Plans
2 Elevations West and South
3 Elevations North and Rear
4 Sections and details

SEATING

EAVES COVE

NORTH END ELEVATION:

SCALE of FEET:

METRIC

EAST (REAR) ELEVATION:

Erected 1839

SHAKER SCHOOL EAST AND NORTH ELEVATIONS

Shaker Village Community School; Lebanon Columbia County.

NAME OF STRUCTURE AND LOCATION

HISTORIC BUILDINGS SURVEY
SHEET 3 OF 4 SHEETS

BUILDING S.S. Center and Church Ga.

HISTORIC COLLECTION NO

3

A. F. Matty, mal it dit.
Troy N.Y. Animber two.

NEW YORK STATE MUSEUM
HISTORIC COLLECTION

DETAILS OF EAVES VERGE AND GABLES:

PROFILE OF EAVES:

EXPOSED END:

EXPOSED SIDE:

SECTION OF GABLE VERGE:

DETAILS OF WINDOWS:

Section of Window

PEG RAIL ROUND SCHOOL ROOM ETC.

LOWER PEG RAIL ROUND ENTRANCE

TYPICAL PEG

PART LONG SECTION LOOKING WEST:

Attic Storage:

Class Room

TEACHERS PLATFORM

Upper School Room

Lower School Room

CROSS SECTION LOOKING SOUTH:

Attic Storage

Upper School Room

Lower School Room

Erected 1839

SECTIONS AND GENERAL DETAILS:

Shaker Village Community School Lebanon Columbia County N.Y.

BUILDING S.F. Center on Church.

A.K. Morley mens et delt. TROY, N.Y. September 1940

NEW YORK STATE MUSEUM HISTORIC COLLECTION

NAME OF STRUCTURE AND LOCATION

HISTORIC BUILDINGS SURVEY
SHEET 4 OF 4 SHEETS

FOR SCHEDULE DRAWINGS SHEET 3

## SISTERS' WORKSHOP: SOUTH FAMILY
## MOUNT LEBANON, NEW YORK

The irregular limestone wall, up to the second floor, is covered with a smooth-finish cement coat. The eight-point, curved doorway is an unusual and beautiful feature in Shaker architecture. The off-center double doors are framed by this arch. The remainder of the building is of wood.

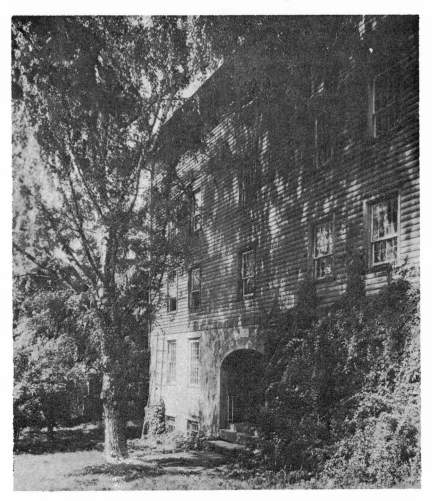

*Sisters' Workshop*

On the left of the main entrance is the dairy room with special arch kettles and sinks; on the right is the laundry with its battery of arch kettles. An unbroken stair rail runs from the first floor to the attic.

The carved stone over the front entrance gives the date of construction as 1851.

SECTION THRU' DOORWAY etc.

TOP OF PLATE
WINDOW HEAD
WINDOW SEAT
ATTIC FLOOR
WINDOW HEAD
WINDOW SEAT
THIRD FLOOR
WINDOW HEAD
WINDOW SEAT
SECOND FLOOR
WINDOW HEAD
WINDOW SEAT
FIRST FLOOR
WINDOW HEAD
WINDOW SEAT
CELLAR FLOOR

RIDGE
CHIMNEY TOP

BOARD SIDING

1851.

UNEXCAVATED

NOTE: CELLAR 8½" FLOOR STONE WALLS PLASTERED OVER

Finished Basement
one room 18' x 22' 9"
one room 18' x 10' 9"

RIDGE
TOP OF PLATE
ATTIC FLOOR
THIRD FLOOR
SECOND FLOOR
FIRST FLOOR
CELLAR BOTTOM

SCALE, N°1:- ¼"=1'-0"
0 1 2 3 4 5 6 7 8 9 10
METRIC SCALE
0 1 2

BUILDING N° 6
HISTORIC BUILDINGS SURVEY
SHEET 1 OF 7 SHEETS

· WEST · ELEVATION ·

LAUNDRY AND SISTERS' CHAIR-MAKING WORKSHOP

NAME OF STRUCTURE AND LOCATION

South Family of Shakers, Lebanon,
COLUMBIA COUNTY, N.Y.

DRAWN BY L.G.WINDS, A.R.Morley Feb. 1945 Nov. 1944
NEW YORK STATE MUSEUM
HISTORIC COLLECTION

NORTH WEST · ELEVATION ·

LAUNDRY and SISTERS CHAIRMAKING WORKSHOP

South Family of Shakers Lebanon, Columbia County N.Y.

BUILDING No 6

HISTORIC BUILDINGS SURVEY
SHEET 2 OF 7 SHEETS

NAME OF STRUCTURE AND LOCATION

NEW YORK STATE MUSEUM
HISTORIC COLLECTION

L.S.WANDS, DEL.

Feb. 1945

NOTE:- CELLAR & FIRST FLOOR
STONE WALL PLASTERED OVER.

BOARD SIDING

SCALE:⅛" = 1'-0"

METRIC SCALE

SOUTH ELEVATION

LAUNDRY AND SISTERS' CHAIR-MAKING WORKSHOP

South Family of Shakers Lebanon COLUMBIA COUNTY N.Y.

BUILDING No. 6.

BOARD SIDING

NOTE: 1st FLOOR STONEWALL PLASTERED OVER

LIGHTLY CONSTRUCTED WOODEN BRIDGE TO THE SUGAR SHOPS

WINDOW HEAD
WINDOW SEAT
ATTIC FLOOR
WINDOW HEAD
WINDOW SEAT
THIRD FLOOR
WINDOW HEAD
WINDOW SEAT
SECOND FLOOR
WINDOW HEAD
WINDOW SEAT
FIRST FLOOR

TOP OF CHIMNEY
RIDGE
TOP OF PLATE
ATTIC FLOOR
THIRD FLOOR
SECOND FLOOR
FIRST FLOOR
CELLAR FLOOR

SCALE, No. 1:- ¼" = 1'-0"
METRIC SCALE

③

NAME OF STRUCTURE AND LOCATION

HISTORIC BUILDINGS SURVEY
SHEET 3 OF 7 SHEETS

L. G. WANDS, DEL.
NEW YORK STATE MUSEUM
HISTORIC COLLECTION

· EAST · ELEVATION ·

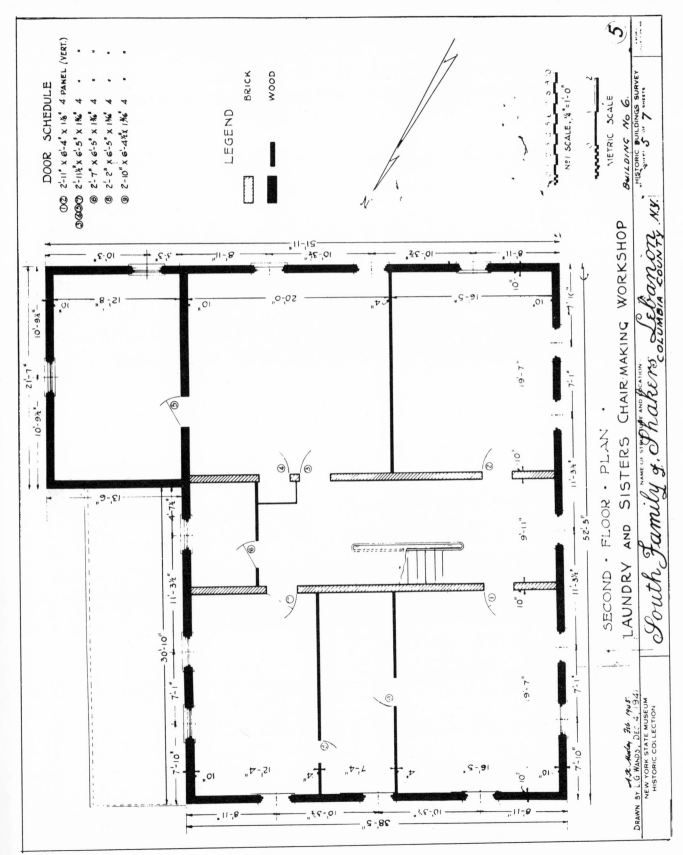

· SECOND · FLOOR · PLAN ·

LAUNDRY AND SISTERS CHAIR-MAKING WORKSHOP

South Family of Shakers, Lebanon, N.Y.

COLUMBIA COUNTY

BUILDING No. 6.

HISTORIC BUILDINGS SURVEY

SHEET 5 OF 7 SHEETS

DRAWN BY L.G. WANDS, DEC. 4, 1941

A.R. Morley, Feb. 1945

NAME OF STRUCTURE AND LOCATION

NEW YORK STATE MUSEUM

HISTORIC COLLECTION

DOOR SCHEDULE

①② 2'-11" X 6'-4" X 1⅜" 4 PANEL (VERT.)

②③④⑦ 2'-11½" X 6'-5" X 1¾" 4 " "

⑤ 2'-7" X 6'-5" X 1¾" 4 " "

⑧ 2'-2" X 6'-5" X 1¾" 4 " "

⑨ 2'-10" X 6'-4¾ X 1⅞" 4 " "

LEGEND

BRICK

WOOD

N° I SCALE, ¼" = 1'-0"

METRIC SCALE

DOOR SCHEDULE
① 2'-6" x 5'-8" x 1¾"    4 PANEL
② 1'-6" x 5'-8" x 1⅜"    2 PANEL
③ 3'-2" x 6'-5" x 1¼"    4 PANEL

LEGEND
STONE
BRICK

N

UNEXCAVATED

UNEXCAVATED

ROOM PLASTERED

UP

STONE FLOOR

· CELLAR · PLAN ·

SCALE N⁰ 1, ¼" = 1'-0"

METRIC SCALE

HISTORIC BUILDINGS SURVEY
SHEET    OF    SHEETS

NAME OF STRUCTURE AND LOCATION

DRAWN BY L.G.WANDS, Nov. 25, 1941.
NEW YORK STATE MUSEUM
HISTORIC COLLECTION

SCHEDULE
OF
DRAWINGS

1  Front West Elevation.
2  North End      "    "
3  South End      "    "
4  First Floor Plan.
5  Second    "    "
6  Third     "    "
7  Cross Section and
   Schedule of Drawings.

0 1 2 3 4 5 6 7 8 9 10
SCALE, Nº 1  ¼"=1'-0"

0        1        2
METRIC SCALE

BUILDING No. 6.
HISTORIC BUILDINGS SURVEY
SHEET 7 OF 7 SHEETS
COLLECTION →

⑦

· CROSS · SECTION ·

LAUNDRY AND SISTERS' CHAIR MAKING WORKSHOP

NAME OF STRUCTURE AND COLLECTION

South Family of Shakers Lebanon N.Y.
COLUMBIA COUNTY
NAME OF STRUCTURE AND LOCATION

A.R. Hurd, Tel. Mus
DRAWN BY L.G.WANDS, DEC. 26, 1941.
NEW YORK STATE MUSEUM
HISTORIC COLLECTION

CHIMNEY TOP
RIDGE
TOP OF PLATE
WINDOW HEAD
WINDOW SEAT
ATTIC FLOOR
WINDOW HEAD
WINDOW SEAT
THIRD FLOOR
WINDOW HEAD
WINDOW SEAT
SECOND FLOOR
WINDOW HEAD
WINDOW SEAT
FIRST FLOOR
WINDOW HEAD
WINDOW SEAT
CELLAR FLOOR

4'-0"
6'-7½"
2'-0"
2'-9¾"
5'-9¾"
4'-3½"
8'-5½"
1'-11½"
8'-5½"
4'-3½"
1'-11½"
5'-3½"
9'-8"
5'-0½"
2'-0"
8'-5"
5'-7"
15'-6"
51'-9"
36'-3"

TOP OF PLATE
FIRST FLOOR
BOTTOM OF SILL
CELLAR FLOOR
BOTTOM

4'-0"
6'-7½"
32'-4¾"
9"
7'-6"
33'-1¾"
51'-5"

*In the Sisters' Sewing Room*

*MAIN DWELLING HOUSE: WEST FAMILY*
*WATERVLIET, NEW YORK*

A painted strip of tin, on the upper floor of this building and over the stairs, gives the date of construction as 1828. Of all the Shaker buildings still remaining at Watervliet (Niskayuna), New York, this is perhaps the most typical example of Shaker architectural design. There are three main floors: an attic, a basement, and a storage cellar.

In the basement are the kitchen, bakeroom, dining room, and food storage rooms or pantries.

On the second floor of the rear extension is the Family Meeting Room. In the attics of both the main structure and this extension are built-in chests

*Main Dwelling House*

of drawers for the storage of clothing and bedding, and a special arrangement of peg boards to hold clothing and hats.

The retiring rooms, or bedrooms, are identical on all floors of the main portion of the structure. The original hand-forged hardware on all the doors is still intact. All woodwork, built-in cupboards, and built-in chests of drawers remain in pristine condition.

Surmounting the slate roof of the main portion of the building is a bell tower approximately 6 feet high and 4 feet square. This bell summoned the members at rising time (4:30 A.M. during the summer and autumn months, and 5:30 A.M. during the winter months), and to the three meals of the day.

The building is of red brick on a foundation of irregular slabs of field stone. The window arches are of brick, and the window sills of limestone.

*Off-Center Double Doors*

BASEMENT · PLAN
SCALE · ⅛"=1'-0"

CELLAR · PLAN
SCALE · ⅛"=1'-0"

GENERAL NOTES:
THE TWO STAIRWAYS FROM THE BASEMENT TO THE FIRST FLOOR IN THE MAIN
BUILDING HAVE BEEN REMOVED AND REPLACED BY A SINGLE STAIRWAY IN THE
EXTENSION, AT THE SAME TIME THE STUD PARTITIONS AND THE STAIRWAY TO
THE CELLAR IN THE EXTENSION WERE ADDED.

DOOR SCHEDULE
CELLAR
① ② 4'-1"×6'-3"×2" BATTEN

FIRST FLOOR
① ② ⑨ ⑯ 2'-10"×6'-5"×1¾" 5 PANEL-1 PANEL GLASS
③ ⑤ ⑥ ⑦ ⑧ ⑪ ⑮ ⑰ 2'-7"×6'-5"×1⅜" 4 PANEL
④ ⑩ ⑫ ⑬ ⑭ 2'-11"×6'-5"×1⅜" "
⑬ ⑭ 2'-11"×6'-5"×1⅜" "
⑳ ㉑ 2'-9"×6'-5" OPENING

UNEXCAVATED

LEGEND
▨ STONE
▨ BRICK
■ WOOD CONST.

G. WILLOUGHBY ALLEN DEL. OCT. 1940
NEW YORK STATE MUSEUM
HISTORIC COLLECTION

NAME OF STRUCTURE AND LOCATION
WEST FAMILY OF WATERVLIET SHAKERS
TOWN OF COLONIE      ALBANY COUNTY N.Y.

BUILDING NO. 1

HISTORIC BUILDINGS SURVEY
SHEET 1 OF 10 SHEETS

SCALE ⅛"=1'-0"
METRIC SCALE

— FIRST · FLOOR · PLAN —
SCALE · ⅛" = 1'-0"

— SECOND · FLOOR · PLAN —
SCALE · ⅛" = 1'-0"

MEETING ROOM

BED ROOM

HALL

LEGEND
BRICK
WOOD CONST.

DOOR SCHEDULE
MAIN BUILDING 1ST FLOOR

GENERAL NOTES.
DOUBLE STAIRWAY IN MAIN BUILDING BETEEN BASEMENT AND
FIRST FLOOR HAS BEEN REMOVED AND REPLACED BY A SINGEE
STAIRWAY IN THE REAR EXTENSION.

G. WILLOUGHBY ALLEN DEL. OCT. 1940
NEW YORK STATE MUSEUM
HISTORIC COLLECTION

NAME OF STRUCTURE AND LOCATION
WEST FAMILY OF WATERVLIET SHAKERS
TOWN OF COLONIE        ALBANY COUNTY N.Y.

BUILDING NO.1

HISTORIC BUILDINGS SURVEY
SHEET 2 OF 10 SHEETS

SCALE ⅛" = 1'-0"

METRIC SCALE

MOULD ON RAKE

ON RAKE OF CORNICE

EXTENSION CORNICE
SCALE 1½"-3"-1-0"  ¾"

BLINDS
FULL SIZE

WINDOW SCALE

MAIN-CORNICE
SCALE N°1-3"=1-0"
1-1"

ON RAKE OF CORNICE

— EAST · ELEVATION —
SCALE N°2-⅛"=1-0"

RIDGE
GARRET FLOOR
ATTIC FLOOR
THIRD FLOOR
SECOND FLOOR
FIRST FLOOR
BASEMENT

SCUTTLE

ATTIC

SLATE ROOF

BELL TOWER
SLATE ROOF
G GUTTER
STONE WINDOW SILLS
BRICK ARCHES
SLATE ROOF
ROOF COND
STONE
BRICK

— WEST · ELEVATION —
SCALE N°2-⅛"=1-0"

SCALE N°1-3"=1-0"
SCALE N°2-⅛"=1-0"

METRIC SCALE

HISTORIC BUILDINGS SURVEY
SHEET 4 OF 10 SHEETS

NAME OF STRUCTURE AND LOCATION
WEST FAMILY OF WATERVLIET SHAKERS
TOWN OF COLONIE     ALBANY COUNTY N.Y.

BUILDING NO. I

G. WILLOUGHBY ALLEN DEL.  NOV. 1940
NEW YORK STATE MUSEUM
HISTORIC COLLECTION

SHEET 6 OF 10 SHEETS

METRIC SCALE

HISTORIC BUILDINGS SURVEY

NAME OF STRUCTURE AND LOCATION

**WEST FAMILY OF WATERVLIET SHAKERS**
TOWN OF COLONIE
ALBANY COUNTY N.Y.

BUILDING NO. 1

G. WILLOUGHBY ALLEN DEL. NOV. 1940.
NEW YORK STATE MUSEUM
HISTORIC COLLECTION

— NORTH · ELEVATION —
SCALE Nº 2-¼"=1'-0"

CROSS SECTION OF BELL TOWER
SCALE Nº 1-¾"=1'-0"

SIDE ELEVATION

FRONT ELEVATION

PLAN

STONE WINDOW SILLS

BRICK ARCHES

BRICK - FLEMISH BOND - 9 COURSES = 24"

CHIMNEY TOP
RIDGE
GARRET FL.
ATTIC FL.
3RD FLOOR
2ND FLOOR
1ST FLOOR
BASEMENT FL.

CHIMNEY TOP
RIDGE
ATTIC FL.
2ND FLOOR
1ST FLOOR
BASEMENT FL.
CELLAR FLOOR

SLATE ROOF
GUTTER
4½ ROOF CONDUCTOR
SLATE ROOF
STONE

CROSS SECTION OF EXTENSION
SCALE N° 2: ⅛"=1'-0"

RIDGE
ATTIC FLOOR
2ND FLOOR
1ST FLOOR
BASEMENT FL.
CELLAR FL.

ROOF PITCH
12"

ROUND

SQUARE

CORNERS CHAMFERED

NEWEL POST
FULL SIZE

DOTTED LINE INDICATES
SKIRTING AROUND
STAIR WELL OPENING

STAIR STRINGER [FULL SIZE]

PLAN
DOWN
UP

12"

PEG RAIL IN END OF ATTIC

BELL ROPE

REMOVED

MAIN BLDG. — EXTENSION —

CROSS · SECTION —
SCALE N° 2: ⅛"=1'-0"

RIDGE
GARRET FL. ROOF PITCH
ATTIC FL.
3RD FL.
2ND FL.
1ST FL.
BASEMENT FL.

STAIR DETAILS
SCALE N° 1: 1¼"=1'-0"

HAND RAIL 2"φ

30¾" ABOVE FLOOR

2.92

6"

30¾"

10"

NOTE:
THE STAIRWAY FROM THE FIRST FLOOR TO THE BASE-
MENT IN THE MAIN BUILDING HAS BEEN REMOVED
AND PLACE IN THE EXTENSION AS SHOWN.

G. WILLOUGHBY ALLEN DEL. NOV. 1940

NEW YORK STATE MUSEUM
HISTORIC COLLECTION:

NAME OF STRUCTURE AND LOCATION
WEST FAMILY OF WATERVLIET SHAKERS
TOWN OF COLONIE          ALBANY COUNTY N.Y.

BUILDING NO. I

HISTORIC BUILDINGS SURVEY
SHEET 7 OF 10 SHEETS

SCALE N° 1: 1¼"=1'-0"
SCALE N° 2: ⅛"=1'-0"
METRIC SCALE

ROOF PITCH
12
2/19

3"×5"×2.3" O.C.
6"×8"

PEG RAIL "
PEGS 10" O.C.

6"×9"

1⅛" ROD

6×13

ROOF TRUSS OVER EXTENSION
SCALE-№2-1½"=1'-0"

8"×9½"
3'-6"
5'-0"

OVEN

OVEN FRONT
SCALE №1-½"=1'-0"

HINGE

CATCH

5"⌀

3"⌀
6"    10"    3"

ROOF CONDUCTOR HEAD
SCALE-1½"=1'-0"

DOOR LATCH
SCALE-6"=1'-0"

SCALE №1-½"=1'-0"
0    1    2    3    4    5    6

SCALE №2-6"=1'-0"
0    1    2    3    4    5    6    7    8

METRIC-SCALE
0    5    10    15    20    25
0    1    2    3    4    5    6

HISTORIC BUILDINGS SURVEY
SHEET 8 OF 10 SHEETS

ATTIC-PLAN
SCALE №2-⅛"=1'-0"

SCUTTLE 2'-0"×3'-0"
DOWN UP
UP UP
ROOF RAFTERS 3×5-3'-0" O.C.

LONGITUDINAL · SECTION · MAIN · BUILDING
SCALE №2-⅛"=1'-0"

TOP OF BELL TOWER
CHIMNEY TOP
RIDGE
GARRET FL.
ATTIC
3RD FL.
2ND FL.
1ST FL.
BASEMENT FL.

WEST FAMILY OF WATERVLIET SHAKERS
ALBANY COUNTY N.Y
TOWN OF COLONIE

NAME OF STRUCTURE AND LOCATION

BUILDING NO. I

G.WILLOUGHBY ALLEN DEL.    DEC. 1940
NEW YORK STATE MUSEUM
HISTORIC COLLECTION

HALL SIDE

DOOR · DETAILS
SCALE · Nº 2 FULL · SIZE

TYPICAL INTERIOR DOOR
HALL SIDE    ROOM SIDE
SCALE Nº 1 ½"=1'-0"

SCALE Nº 1  ½"=1'-0"
SCALE Nº 2 FULL SIZE
METRIC SCALE

DOOR · HARDWARE
SCALE · 6"=1'-0"

FL.
BASE

6¾"

SILL

WOOD · THUMB · SCREW

DOTTED · LINE · INDICATES
MUNTIN

STONE WINDOW SILL

WOOD THUMB
SCREWS ON RIGHT
SIDE ONLY TO FAST-
EN SASH STOP

TYPICAL WINDOW
INTERIOR
EXTERIOR
SCALE · Nº 1 · ½"=1'-0"

STOP
THUMB SCREW

DOTTED LINE INDICATES
WINDOW HEAD

JAMB

WINDOW · DETAILS
SCALE · Nº 2 FULL SIZE

MEETING · RAIL

G. WILLOUGHBY ALLEN DEL.    DEC. 1940
NEW YORK STATE MUSEUM
HISTORIC COLLECTION

NAME OF STRUCTURE AND LOCATION
WEST FAMILY OF WATERVLIET SHAKERS
ALBANY COUNTY N.Y.
TOWN OF COLONIE

BUILDING NO. I

HISTORIC BUILDINGS SURVEY
SHEET 9 OF 10 SHEETS

SECTION "A"
SCALE Nº 2 FULL SIZE

SECTION "B"
SCALE Nº 2 FULL SIZE

2'-4½" TO FLUE
20"
16½"
2'-4½"

SECTION

2'-0"

BRICK

ELEVATION

ARCH KETTLES
IN ROOM OFF THE
KITCHEN IN THE
BASEMENT.

2'-0"

24" Ø

PLAN
SCALE Nº 1-½"=1'-0"

¼" THICK IRON

FLUE

PLAN    SECTION

5½"

HINGE

LATCH
SCALE 6"=1'-0"

CATCH

SCALE Nº 1  1  2  ¹ C⁴

SCALE Nº 2 FULL SIZE

METRIC SCALE

HISTORIC BUILDINGS SURVEY
SHEET 10 OF 10 SHEETS

TYPICAL CHEST OF DRAWS
SCALE Nº 1-½"=1'-0

3'-9"

5'-11"

CHEST OF DRAWS
SCALE Nº 2 FULL SIZE

CHEST OF DRAWS [1st FL. EXTENSION]

3'-5½"

2'-0½"

3'-5½"

3'-10½"

SECTION "C"
SCALE Nº 2 FULL SIZE.

19½"

DOVETAILS
ABOUT 1½ O.C.

FRONT

SIDE

BACK

NAME OF STRUCTURE AND LOCATION
WEST FAMILY OF WATERVLIET SHAKERS
TOWN OF COLONIE        ALBANY COUNTY N.Y.

BUILDING NO. I

G.WILLOUGHBY ALLEN DEL. DEC. 1940
NEW YORK STATE MUSEUM
HISTORIC COLLECTION

Key Plan of Hancock Shaker Village.

20 DORMITORY
19 LAUNDRY AND
18 STORE MACHINE
16 DAIRY 17 WOOD SHOP
15 BROTHERS SHOP
13 STORES 14 BARN
12 AUTO GARAGE
11 ICE HOUSE
10 TANNERY
7-8-9 HORSES, YOUNG STOCK · WAGONS
6 FODDER & WAGONS
5 MILK CATTLE
4 ROUND BARN
3 MINISTRY & SHOP
2 FAMILY RESIDENCE
1 TRUSTEES & OFFICE

OUTLINE ELEVATION AS SEEN FROM THE ALBANY TO PITTSFIELD OLD POST ROAD.

Memo: This Hancock Shakers had a very efficient water supply from Reservoir placed higher up the Mountain to the North.

Building No 19 for example has 12 inch cast iron water main, utilizing pressure to operate a 12 inch Turbine furnishing ample power for this large Building containing LAUNDRY with Machines on Private Shops.

A separate 6 inch Turbine serves which a smaller power only is requisite.

CROSS SECTION OF CATTLE BARN.

Memo: This Hancock Shakers was organized between 1790 and 1790. The Round Stone Barn was built 1826 but about 1870 was accidentally burnt out. This framing of the structure was replaced by new. More recently a new Cattle Shed was erected to the south to furnish large accommodation and to avoid reconstructing the cattle floor with reinforced concrete as required by the new Sanitary Code of the State of Massachusetts.

A. F. Marley
Troy N.Y.

NEW YORK STATE MUSEUM
HISTORIC COLLECTION

Hancock Shakers Round Stone Cattle Barn

NAME OF STRUCTURE AND LOCATION:
Hancock Shakers Round Stone Cattle Barn

BUILT West Pittsfield Mass.
1826

SCALE to MAIN CROSS SECTION only

HISTORIC BUILDINGS SURVEY
SHEET 1 OF 2 SHEETS

About 90 feet diameter outside External Walls

HAY STORAGE

INDICATING KEY TO CONSTRUCTION

INDICATING 2 WAY CONSTRUCTION

INDICATING 2 WAY SKELETON BRACINGS

WACONS and DRIVE WAY

CATTLE STANCHIONS ETC NOW REMOVED

Basement Manure Storage

Dooryway with Arched Stone Head dated 1826

### ROUND BARN: HANCOCK SHAKERS, WEST PITTSFIELD, MASSACHUSETTS

The stones of the large curved-arch doorway bear the date 1826. Tradition and Shaker folklore say that one of the brethren, who was wheelwright and cooper, suggested that this barn should have a circular floor plan. The floor plan and elevation of this W.P.A. drawing shows that there are three concentric elements and that they are of different heights.

The central, or the innermost, element is octagonal which, on the interior forms a skeletal framework, allows free circulation of air through it from the basement and out through the louvered cupola. This lessened the danger of spontaneous combustion. The center element is for the storage of hay

*Round Barn*

which is filled from the second floor of the first element and has a driveway around its entire circumference, allowing the cattle to feed from this perpetual self-leveling hay mow.

On the first floor of the first, or outermost, element are the cattle stanchions and the unique trap doors, located at intervals in the sunken circular trough. These trap doors allow the manure to be shoved down into the basement and piled in heaps under each door.

In the basement of this building a large door admitted a wagon that encircled the basement for the loading of the manure already stacked in heaps under the trap doors.

The diameter of the entire structure is about ninety feet, and the circumference about two-hundred feet. The exterior element is of field stone and the other two elements are of wood.

The initial cost of the Hancock Round Barn was $800. About 1884 the interior of this structure was gutted by fire started by an overturned lantern. All frame material had to be reconstructed.